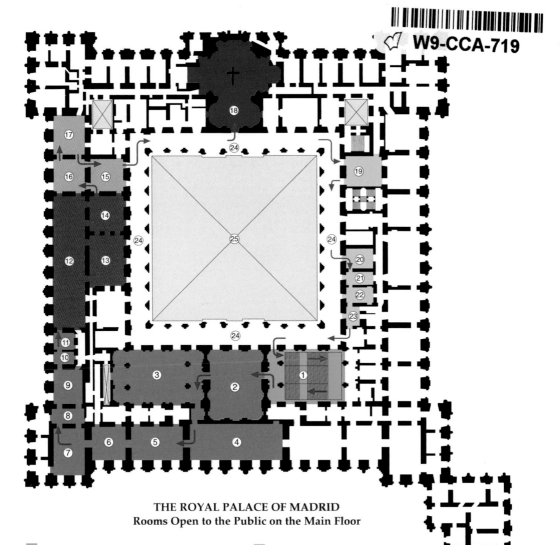

THE ROYAL PALACE OF MADRID
Rooms Open to the Public on the Main Floor

1 **Main Staircase**

KING CHARLES III'S APARTMENTS
2 **Halberdiers' Room**
3 **Hall of Columns**
4 **Throne Room**
5 **Charles III's Anteroom (Saleta)**
6 **Charles III's Chamber Antechamber**
7 **Charles III's Chamber or the Gasparini Room**
8 **Charles III's 'Tram' Room**
9 **Charles III's Hall**
10 **Porcelain Room**
11 **Yellow Room**

THE QUEEN'S APARTMENTS
12 **Banqueting Hall**
13 **Plateresque or Band Room**
14 **Silverware Room**

THE APARTMENTS OF THE INFANTE DON LUIS
15 **Chinaware Room**

16 **Stradivarius Room**
17 **Musical Instruments Room**

18 **Royal Chapel**

BACK-ROOMS OF QUEEN MARÍA LUISA
19 **Guardroom of Queen María Luisa or Antechamber of Queen María Cristina**
20 **Alfonso XII's Billiard Room**
21 **Smoking Room or Japanese Room of Alfonso XII**
22 **Stucco Room of Queen María Luisa**
23 **Fine Woods Room of Queen María Luisa**

24 **Main Gallery**

25 **Palace's Courtyard**

PALACIO REAL
DE MADRID

JOSÉ LUIS SANCHO

REALES SITIOS DE ESPAÑA

© PATRIMONIO NACIONAL, 2004
Palacio Real de Madrid
Bailén, s/n
28071 Madrid
Tel. 91 547 53 50

Text: José Luis Sancho Gaspar

Photographs: Patrimonio Nacional.
Félix Lorrio, José Barea, Gerardo Romera,
Antonio Sanz, Ramón Guerra

N.I.P.O.: 006-04-006-5
I.S.B.N.: 84-7120-294-8
Legal Deposit: M-13292-2004

Co-ordination and production: ALDEASA
Layout: Myriam López Consalvi
Translation: Mervyn Samuel
Correction: Philip Knight
Photograph setting: Lucam
Printed: Estudios Gráficos Europeos

Photograph on the Front Cover: A view of the Western Façade of the Royal Palace of Madrid from the Fountain of Shells in the Campo del Moro Park.

Photograph on the Inside Cover: The workshop of G.D. Olivieri: The Royal Coat of Arms flanked by griffins. Colmenar stone. The Crown in the balustrade of the central section on the Eastern Façade. The Royal Palace of Madrid.

Printed in Spain

Contents

ATRIMONIO NACIONAL (National Heritage) is
the institution which manages those properties
of the State which are at the service of the
Crown for performing representative functions
as commended by the Constitution and Laws
of Spain.

The institution manages a number of
palaces, as well as several Monasteries and
Convents founded by Spanish monarchs, all of
great historical, artistic and cultural importance
and, most significantly, of great symbolic
value. The Royal Palaces of Madrid, El Pardo,
Aranjuez, San Ildefonso and La Almudaina are
used as residential and representative
buildings as was intended when they were
built centuries ago and it is here where His
Majesty the King performs his duties as Head
of State, particularly in the Royal Palace of
Madrid, where this symbolic value is felt most
strongly, as the official residence of the Crown.

In harmony with these functions, the other
buildings and properties which make up
Patrimonio Nacional have a decidedly cultural
purpose and are places of study and research,
as well as being open to the general public.

Both the buildings and the Spanish royal
collections (27 in all, ranging from fans to tools
and which include silverware, paintings,
tapestries, furniture, musical instruments,
clocks, etc.) are remarkable for a number of
characteristics which go to make Patrimonio
Nacional a unique cultural institution: their
particular purpose, as they are still considered
valid for representative use by the Crown; their
historical authenticity, as they are all pieces
which have been ordered, acquired or offered
as gifts at some time for that particular place;
their originality, which can be seen by the

absence of replicas and imitations, and their
extraordinary artistic, historical and
symbolic value.

The combination of such impressive
characteristics makes it clear to the visitor that
Patrimonio Nacional is much more than a
simple museum.

The Spanish Royal Palaces are surrounded
by approximately 20,500 hectares of open land.
Around 500 hectares are given over to gardens
or farmland, while the remaining 20,000
hectares are forest, divided between El Pardo,
La Herrería and Riofrío and part of which is
open to the general public. These woodlands,
mainly of the biotype Mediterranean forest, are
of renowned ecological importance, the value
of which is at a par with the monuments found
in their midst.

The Royal Monasteries and Convents have
been attended by the same religious orders
since their foundation, with the exception of
San Lorenzo de El Escorial, originally of the
Hieronymite Order, which was passed over to
the Augustinian Order following the sale of
Church lands in the 19th century. They enjoy
particular importance in the history of Spain, as
their origin dates back to the particular
patronage of the monarchs of the era.

By being open to the general public, not
only do these buildings fulfil a cultural
purpose, they allow the Spanish people to
capture their symbolic value, identify with it
and consider themselves a legatee of the vast
historical and artistic treasures which make up
the properties of Patrimonio Nacional.

Collected over the centuries by the Crown,
their influence in the cultural identity of Spain
has been, and still is, decisive.

8

▲ *Top Left*. The Alcázar, Madrid; *Right*. El Escorial Monastery. *Below Left*. The Palace of El Pardo. *Right*. Aranjuez Palace. *Michel-ange Houasse: Details from the series of* Views of the Royal Residences. Eighteenth century.

Introduction

From Fortress to Palace

THE ROYAL Palace is on the site where once stood the Alcázar of Madrid, the "famous castle" built at the end of the 9th century, during the reign of Mohammed I, Emir of Córdoba, as a key position for the defence of these territories situated to the north of Toledo.

The fortress, rebuilt in the 14th century, began to acquire the character of a royal residence with the work undertaken by John II, particularly the chapel consecrated in 1434, and the great 'Sala Rica' (Luxurious Hall). It was in the 16th century that Charles V and Philip II rebuilt it as a Royal Palace, so that in 1561 the Alcázar became the permanent residence of the Kings, and the "villa" or town of Madrid which arose under the protection of its castle became the Court of the Spanish Monarchy. Under Philip IV, the Palace of Madrid attained its most characteristic form: on the exterior, with the long façade designed by Francisco and Juan Gómez de Mora and G. B. Crescenci; on the interior, with the participation of Diego Velázquez as interior-design architect and with the display of masterpieces which today are the pride of the Prado Museum. Philip V also left his mark on the Alcázar before the greatest and best part of its structure disappeared in a fire on the Christmas Eve of 1734.

The location of the Alcázar and its groundplan, conceived around the buildings containing the living quarters, in such a way conditioned the shape of the New Royal Palace and its setting that we could almost claim that it is still present today, eleven centuries on, despite the disappearance of all visible remains in the area.

The Royal Seats

The fact that Madrid, and more accurately the Alcázar or Royal Palace, was the seat of power, did not mean that the King lived only in this Palace. Quite the contrary, the game reserves near Madrid used by the Trastamara dynasty (El Pardo, Valsaín), the domain of Aranjuez incorporated into the Crown by the Catholic Monarchs, the Monastery of El Escorial founded by Philip II, and other possessions also created by the latter Monarch (especially the neighbouring Casa de Campo, on the other side of the Manzanares), constituted a system of "Royal Seats" defined at the time when the capital was established here. During the following three centuries it was extended and improved with new Royal Seats, such as The Buen Retiro and La Granja de San Ildefonso, creations of Philip IV and Philip V respectively. The use of these residences was seasonal, according to their nature and characteristics: springtime was spent at Aranjuez, summer at Valsaín (from the time of Philip V at the nearby La Granja), autumn at El Escorial... The Monarchs stayed in Madrid from the end of October until Holy Week, but with prolonged stays at the winter hunting lodge of El Pardo. Philip V, and particularly Charles III, took this systematic absence from the capital to its ultimate consequences. This system did not always function in a strict manner, but though it was subject to exceptions, novelties and changes imposed by the preferences of each Monarch, the fact is that for three centuries it governed the life of the Spanish Court, the main axis of which was the Palace of Madrid.

The New Royal Palace

Therefore, it comes as no surprise that, almost as soon as the fire of that Christmas Eve of 1734 was extinguished, Philip V decided to build a new Royal Palace in Madrid, and to do so on the very same site where the former one had stood, as a symbol of the continuity of the Monarchy. He wanted the entire structure to have stone vaulting, with timber being employed only for doors and window-frames, in order to avoid further fires. There may also have been a desire to identify the solidity of the seat with that of power: the inscription on the foundation stone states that it was built "for eternity". The Palace needed space for all the functions of the Court, one of the most important in Europe at that time. Moreover, this was precisely the moment when ideas regarding the splendour that should surround regal power were reaching their maximum expression.

Architecture: projects and construction

PHILIP V also wanted the architect of his Palace to be the best and most famous one in Europe, and he chose well. At the beginning of 1735, the Italian Filippo Juvarra was summoned to Madrid. He quickly realized that the location of the Alcázar was not appropriate for a residence as large and magnificent as was intended, and he conceived a vast project with horizontal development, much more suitable for a flat site. However, Juvarra died in March 1736, and being delighted with his style the Monarchs decided to call on a disciple of his to build the master's great project.

So it was that G. B. Sacchetti, of Turin, came to Madrid, and was commissioned to "adapt" Juvarra's design to the site of the old Palace, which was no easy matter. He had neither the prestige nor the personality of Juvarra, and as he was in no position to object, he obeyed.

Thus, the final form of the Palace is the result of a complex process, the basic elements of which are the plans of Juvarra, the adaptation of these in what really was a completely new project by Sacchetti, and modifications of many aspects introduced during construction. Finally, there were the changes introduced into the Palace of Sacchetti by Sabatini, architect of Charles III.

The architectural design of the Palace, in its general features and its details, is characteristic of the classical late-Baroque taste of Juvarra, chiefly inspired by the famous Roman artist Bernini, and it follows the lines of the great project that never became a reality. However, Sacchetti had to convert the original horizontal conception into a vertical design so that, occupying the same site as the old Alcázar, the New Palace would be able to accomodate the Royal Family, courtiers, servants, ministries and service quarters. Thus, the building has a minimum of six storeys and a maximum of eight: two basements compensating for the uneven ground on the west and the north, for the "offices of household and mouth" and for secretariat offices. A lower floor for summer quarters of the Royal Family, and a main floor for the winter quarters. A second floor for the lords and ladies-in-waiting, and finally the rooms in the mezzanines over the lower, principal and second floors, for the servants. Given the Royal intention that all the floors were to be vaulted and the building was to be fireproof and abiding, the walls needed to be made extremely thick in order to sustain such pressure.

The general ground-plan of the building did not change from the first plan, dated 9 March 1737; it is square, with a single main Courtyard, also square, in the centre, surrounded by galleries with arcades. The main rooms are arranged in line along the façades, the antechambers and secondary rooms overlook the Courtyard, and between the two ranges of rooms run service corridors. Three small courtyards provide light for the

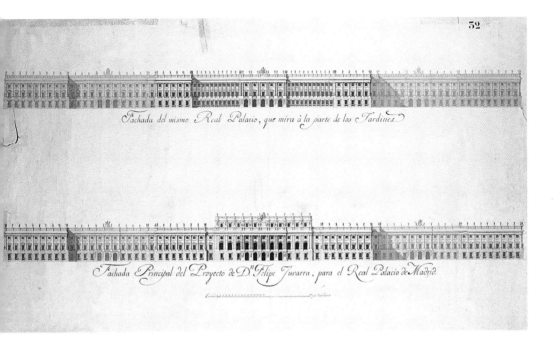

Fachada del mismo Real Palacio, que mira à la parte de los Jardines

Fachada Principal del Proyecto de D.ⁿ Felipe Juvarra, para el Real Palacio de Madrid.

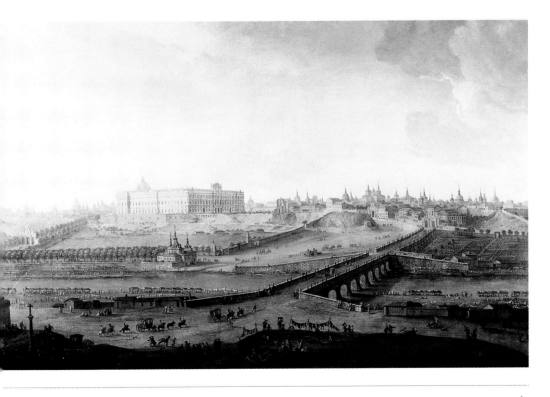

Top. Filippo Juvarra: Main Façade from the Project..., for the Royal Palace of Madrid *and*... the Gardens, 1735. ▲
Below. Antonio Joli: View of Madrid and the New Royal Palace... Eighteenth century. Private Collection.

INTRODUCTION

interior rooms at the corners. Something of the spirit of the Alcázar seems to float about the New Palace, since its manifest solidity, the projections or "towers" at the corners, the escarpment below its walls, its elevation and situation, endow it with the air of a fortress.

Between 1738 and 1747, as work was progressing, Sacchetti made some changes in his plan as a result of criticism from the Secretary to the Queen, Marqués Annibale Scotti, and from some of the architects engaged on the project. In 1742, and due to Scotti's influence, he gave greater importance to the Staircase, which became double with symmetrical twin flights. Between them he left a hall for social gatherings –what is now the Halberdiers' Room– originally intended for the Chapel, now moved to the north side. In this way, it proved possible to harmonize reminiscences of the Alcázar, Sacchetti's obsession with symmetry, and the urge for ostentation of the Spanish Monarchs, who at that time desired the spaces in the Palace to be of the greatest possible magnificence.

Inhabitants of the Palace and changes in decoration

INTERIOR DISTRIBUTION and decoration are two aspects closely linked in a residence, and they usually change simultaneously, according to the needs and tastes of succeeding generations of occupants. Each reign implies different people and preferences, and moreover, ideas concerning the representation of the Royal Majesty were evolving along with social and political changes: there is a chasm between the significance of the person of the King in the Absolute Monarchy, what it became with Liberalism in the 19th century, and what it now is in a parliamentary democracy.

View of the Northern and Western Façades of the Royal Palace of Madrid.

The plans inside the rear cover show the distribution prevailing during each reign. Ferdinand VI did not think about children, which he did not have, and thus his apartments and those of the Queen proved almost as extensive as required by prevailing contemporary ideas about royal residences. Conversely, Charles III had to have large rooms sub-divided, yet still the Palace always seemed small to him, as to his children. In the eyes of succeeding generations it has come to appear larger and larger, even excessive, due to new concepts of comfort that have arisen as a result of progress and which have been reflected in politics and society as a whole.

The decoration conceived under Ferdinand VI by Sacchetti, Giaquinto and other artists was of a rather heavy late-Baroque style, but it also was modified with the arrival of Charles III, who brought with him a relatively more sober, classical taste, largely due to the Sicilian Francesco Sabatini, a disciple and son-in-law of Luigi Vanvitelli, architect of the Palace of Caserta. Sabatini directed all aspects of the interior decoration of the Palace, except when the King's will was to entrust it to others (as in the Throne Room or the suite decorated by Gasparini), and he did this by harmonizing the dignity of the design with the richness of the materials. These included the magnificent Spanish marbles of the jambs and socles, a collection of over three-hundred samples being gathered together in the Palace, and the solid mahogany of all the doors, windows and shutters. Sabatini and his team were responsible for producing the designs of the stuccoes, the furniture and the ornamental bronzes (which for the most part have disappeared), and these were executed by a series of Italian and French masters chosen and recruited by him. During the period of almost forty years of his activity at the Palace, from 1760 to 1797, his taste and that

of his patrons evolved from an attachment to th Rococo towards the forms of classicism.

Together with Sabatini, the artist whose influence was most profound on the decoratio of the New Palace was the painter Anton Raphael Mengs. This was not only because he produced several of his masterpieces here, but

The Eastern Façade of the Royal Palace of Madrid, seen from the Plaza de Oriente Gardens.

so because the high esteem in which he was ield by the King converted him into an artistic ictator, who in order to decorate the maining ceilings freely chose young Spanish ainters and imprinted his personal style on em: Francisco Bayeu and Mariano Salvador aella were the most prominent, displacing

the disciples of Corrado Giaquinto who had been omnipotent in the Palace under Ferdinand VI. Giaquinto, who had created frescoes of great beauty, avoided the tyranny of Mengs and Sabatini whenever he could. Neither did the great Tiepolo, nor his offspring, fare much better with the latter duo.

Under Charles III and Charles IV a fundamental element in the decoration were the pictures that entirely covered the walls from the frieze or socle to the cornice: visitors were perplexed at the combination of such an accumulation of masterpieces and the sumptuous decoration of the Palace. In some rooms tapestries would replace the paintings during the wintertime. However, early in the 19th century tastes changed: at the most, one single picture on a wall was enough, on top of the silk hangings or of the wallpapers that began to be used by then. Thus, Ferdinand VII removed the great majority of the masterpieces that later he brought together in the Royal Painting Gallery, nowadays the Prado Museum.

The appearance of the State Rooms is also decidedly "Ferdinand VII" in style due to other essential features of the furnishings. Charles IV had a passion for French furniture and decorative objects, so that the Royal Collections conserve splendid pieces from that period. This taste was continued by his son Ferdinand VII, who made massive purchases of Parisian bronze objects mainly between 1818 and 1830: clocks, candelabra and chandeliers. Despite their beauty, they are so numerous that it is not possible to offer an extensive description of each one: when no more details are given, they may be assumed to be in the style of Ferdinand VII and from Paris. The effect of rich "Empire-style" profusion that they then produced must have been tremendous, as they were then concentrated in the western half of the Palace, much more so than nowadays when they are dispersed throughout the residence.

The changes in decoration under Isabel II, though important in the eastern half of the building, and particularly in her private rooms, are insignificant compared to those of both her

▲ Left. *F. Juvarra: Console sculpted by B. Steccone, 1736. A detail. Reign of Philip V.*
Right. *G. B. Tiepolo:* Jason and the Golden Fleece. *Vault of the official Antechamber. Reign of Charles III.*

ather and her son, Alfonso XII. The
restoration brought with it a desire to
modernise the Madrid Palace according to
the standards of Victorian royal residences,
within the taste of the late 19th-century
conservative bourgeoisie for dark,
multicoloured interiors. Work was directed by
the architect José Segundo de Lema, and
consisted of preparing and decorating various
adjacent rooms including one to be used as
both a Banqueting Hall and a Ballroom. The
project also included a Billiard Room, a
smoking Room, and the laying of parquet in
many of the private rooms and State Rooms,
into which furnishings in the style of the period
were also introduced. For this purpose, some
important decorative features and frescoes by
Mengs were sacrificed. The 20th century has
been marked by great restoration schemes
carried out after the Spanish Civil War of 1936-
1939, and in recent years.

The visit

The Parade Ground and main façade

ACCESS TO the Royal Palace from the city has
always been by way of Calle Mayor (main street)
and so on to the Royal Armoury. This building,
which was demolished in 1884 and has given its
name to the square existing between the
Cathedral of La Almudena and the Palace, was
located in the area now occupied by the grand
railings which enclose the Parade Ground.

After passing the railings we reach the
Plaza de Palacio, also known as the Plaza de
Armas or Parade Ground because military
parades and ceremonies take place here. Since
the 16th century, this has been the stage for the
Monarch to appear before the people
accompanied by all the pomp and splendour of
the Court, with the main façade of the royal
residence as a backdrop. Sacchetti and Ventura

Left. Glass Chandelier with engraved and gilded bronzes. Manufactured in France. Nineteenth Century. Official Antechamber. ▲
Reign of Ferdinand VII. Right. Tapestry Room. Ornamental set from the reign of Alfonso XII.

Rodríguez conceived this Square with open porticoes to connect the Palace with the auxiliary buildings, but Sabatini gave the space its present character of a French cour d'honneur, enclosed by two prolongations of the royal suites, of which the only one to be finished (in 1783, and its decoration in 1788) was the one on the right side known as the Saint Giles Wing. The left-hand wing never progressed beyond the level of the first floor.

The low pavilions forming the sides of the Square follow the general lines drawn by Sabatini, but they date from the 19th century and, like the grand railings in the French style, they correspond to the project of Narciso Pascual y Colomer (1847), who during the reign of Isabel II completed the one on the right-hand side; the one on the left was built by his successors between 1883 and 1893. The open arches to the left, overlooking the Palace Park, allow us to understand the fascination of this site. On the other side of the river, the Casa de Campo spreads out until linking up with the Monte de El Pardo, and on clear days it is possible to see the Monastery of El Escorial in the distant mountains. The continuity of all these royal properties was even more pronounced while the Royal Seat of La Florida (also known as La Moncloa) existed; it was created by Charles IV, and occupied all of the present-day Argüelles district, in addition to the Western Park and the University Campus.

The forms of the architecture of the Palace, inspired in Bernini and Juvarra, may be observed in detail on the main façade. Above a cushioned base, corresponding to the ground floor and to the first mezzanine, rises a course of giant Ionic columns side -by-side with Tuscan pilasters articulating the main floor, second mezzanine and second floor. The great cornice is surmounted by a balustrade which conceals the lead roofs.

The building was originally given a highly Baroque plasticity and propagandistic sense by the numerous statues carved by a large team of Spanish artists led by the Italian Gian Domenico Olivieri and by Felipe de Castro (from Galicia), the principal sculptors of Ferdinand VI. The statues placed on the surmounting balustrade represented the Kings of Spain, from the first of the Goths to Ferdinand VI; while at the level of the main floor, on the pedestals at the corners, there were pairs of Suevian Kings, Counts of Castile, Kings of Navarre, Aragón and Portugal pre-Columbian Emperors and two Patron Saints of Spain. This sculptural exuberance increased still further as work progressed, due to the influence of the learned Benedictine monk Fray Martín Sarmiento, who was entrusted with designing the complex iconographic programme. However, it was abruptly suppressed by Charles III, who ordered the removal of all the statues in order to give the building a more classical air. Only with the modern restoration of the façades, concluded in 1973, the statues seen today were replaced. Among the most noteworthy are, at the corners on the main floor level, those of Montezuma, Emperor of Mexico, by Juan Pascual de Mena (left), and the Peruvian Atahualpa by Domingo Martínez.

Where Sabatini placed the four Doric columns, which allowed him to give more projection to the balcony, Ferdinand VI ordered the installation of the statues of four Roman Emperors born in Hispania: Honorius and Theodosius, by Olivieri, and Trajan and Arcadius by Castro; since 1791 they have been in the Prince's Courtyard. Above the balcony, with three large arch-shaped window spaces that were also reduced by Sabatini, the relief of Spain the Arms Bearer of Spain is by Olivieri.

Sabatini also designed the clock on the attic level. One of the two bells of the clock comes

Top. Retinue for the Presentation of Credentials to the King, with entry to the Parade Ground through the Grand Railings.
Below. The Ceremonial Changing of the Royal Guard in the Parade Ground.

from the old Alcázar clock and is dated 1637, while the other bell is dated 1761. When the sphere was installed, Sabatini removed the castle in relief, the sculpture of the lion with the two globes and the Plus Ultra columns, which with the Zodiac (still surviving to the sides) composed a heraldic emblem of the Crown. Statues of the Kings who built the Palace have been returned to the adjoining pedestals.

The Hallway and the Main Staircase

THERE ARE five doorways on the façade: through the two side ones vehicles enter the small vestibules and from there continue to the Main Courtyard. The three central doorways lead to the Main Vestibule or atrium, where Tuscan columns of pink Sepúlveda limestone give a certain warmth to the whiteness of the Colmenar stone. Carriages arriving here leave their occupants (only Monarchs, Heads of State or Ambassadors) at the foot of the Main Staircase on the right-hand side, opposite which stands the statue of Charles III as a Roman general by Pierre Michel.

The two twin main staircases, the one on the right for the King, and that on the left for the Queen, were an idea of the Marqués Scotti, accepted in 1742. Sacchetti conceived them with great magnificence and scenographic display, but he came up against the criticism of Scotti himself and of his protegé Bonavia, who considered the steps too high. The obsession of making the ascent as comfortable as possible motivated a dispute in the Court that gave rise to various projects, including ones of note by Bonavia, one by the important Roman architects Vanvitelli, Fuga and Salvi, and the alternatives put forward by Sacchetti himself during those years, taking ever more space towards the eastern and western façades.

Main Hallway. Pierre Michel: Charles III as a Roman general *–in the niche opposite the staircase.* ▲

Bonavia was the first to propose an open stairwell, without intermediate support, an approach in which he was followed by Sacchetti and by the architects of the Roman Academy of San Luca, consulted in 1746. Fuga, Salvi and Vanvitelli, though approving Sacchetti, nevertheless sent a fine design of their own as an appropriate solution, but as the Monarchs did not like it, the polemic had to be solved at the end of 1746 by the Directors of the nascent Academy of Fine Arts of San Fernando. Sacchetti emerged as the winner with his most ambitious project, and in the following years constructed these two spaces which now are the Main Staircase and the Hall of Columns; but the ramps, the ingenious and theatrical arrangement of which offered nine exits on the main floor, went no further than being constructed in wood, so that the King could see the effect.

However, Charles III did not like either the form Sacchetti had given to the flights of steps or the layout of the Antechambers through which his apartments and those of the Queen were approached, and recalling the staircase of the great Palace of Caserta created in Naples by Vanvitelli, he instructed Sabatini to build a similar single staircase in one of the two stairwells, leaving the other as a ballroom.

Thus, in 1760 Sabatini made the Staircase as we see it today, but on the opposite side, to the left. When Charles IV came to the throne in 1789, he ordered the architect to move it to the right-hand side, as it is now, for the reasons of distribution mentioned above. Sabatini reused the same materials and steps. These consist of single pieces of San Agustín marble. They are very low and wide, so that the rise is extremely gentle, which was important particularly for the sedan chairs used by the ladies to reach the main floor.

The central flight ends in a large landing, where it is advisable to move close to the wall

in order to observe the entire space: the lions are by two different sculptors, the stiffer one by Felipe de Castro, and the more flexible one by Robert Michel, gracefully turning its head.

The four large white vases of Carrara marble, with a bas-relief hunting motif and allegorical trophies, form part of a series of 28 which were sculpted between 1721 and 1728 by Jean Thierry for the Gardens at the San Ildefonso estate. They were to be found there until Charles IV ordered their transfer; the remaining pieces of the series are in Aranjuez.

All the ceiling decoration, which was completed in the lifetime of Ferdinand VI, is the work of Corrado Giaquinto, from whose designs G.B. Andreoli made the stuccoes. The frescoes are Giaquinto's second work in the Palace, after those of the Chapel, and as they were painted when Sacchetti's plan for the staircase was still in force, they are designed to be seen from what was then the main exit, now the Camón gallery, where the seated statue of Charles IV as a Roman Emperor, by Ramón Barba (1817), is now located.

Therefore, it is important to stand close to the wall in order to look at the central allegory representing Religion protected by Spain, and then while ascending the second flight one can see the beautiful figures of Liberality and Public Happiness (to the left), Magnificence and Peace (to the right), in which contemporaries recognized the characteristic virtues of the reign of Ferdinand VI. Hercules lifting up the Pillars of Gibraltar before Neptune in the Camón gallery, above the entrance intended by Sacchetti to lead to the King's Apartments, and The Triumph of Spain over Saracen Power above the doorway to the Halberdiers' Room, along with other small medallions, complete the pictorial decoration.

Here, two anecdotes must inevitably come to mind. One concerns Napoleon, who on his visit to Madrid stopped on the landing, and turning to the new King Joseph exclaimed, "Brother, you

C. Giaquinto. Religion protected by Spain. J. B. Andreoli: Stucco decoration. The vault above the Main Staircase ▶

◀ Main Staircase. A view from the central landing, looking towards the landing on the lower floor.

level of the windows where musicians could be placed. However, Charles III assigned it as a Guard Room, and consequently Sabatini decorated it in the simplest possible manner with Tuscan pilasters, instead of the rich ornamentation it would otherwise have received. Also dating from 1760 is the floor of Colmenar stone and red stone from El Molar; the flagstones were originally intended to pave the Gallery surrounding the Courtyard on this storey; the floor of the Saleta is similar, but is not seen as it is covered by the carpet.

This noble simplicity did not prevent rich pictorial embellishment in the frescoes, where G.B. Tiepolo produced one of his masterpieces, Venus charging Vulcan to forge the arms of Aeneas, a topic inspired in a passage from Virgil's Aeneid and chosen for the military function of the room, though it does seem also to allude to Charles III as a warrior hero, and to his mother Queen Isabella Farnese as the promoter of his Italian conquests.

Until the twentieth century the furnishings of this room were very simple, being limited to benches and other objects for the Halberdiers' use.

On both sides of the fireplace, four of the eight console tables of mahogany and gilded bronze, made between 1793 and 1802 following a design by Francesco Sabatini for the Dining Room or Anteroom of Charles IV, in this same Palace. On them are French clocks and two models, in bronze and hard stones, of the Fountain of the Four Rivers created by Bernini in the Piazza Navona of Rome. The pictures above are two fine 18th-century copies of Sibyls painted by Raphael in the Stanza della Segnatura of the Vatican Palace, and two landscapes with mythological scenes by B.M. Agüero (late 17th century).

On the Courtyard side there are two further console tables from the early 19th century, in carved and gilded wood, though the tops are of

are to have a house much better than mine". The other is the celebrated Battle on the Palace Staircase, the attempted kidnapping of the child Queen Isabel II by General Diego de León and his soldiers, who were opposed by the Halberdiers, under the orders of Colonel Dulce (1841).

At the top of the staircase there are two other important sculptural portraits of Spanish Monarchs of the Bourbon Dynasty, brought here from the Palace of La Granja: Philip V and his second wife Isabella Farnese, by René Frémin, who also designed the splendid marble and bronze pedestals.

King Charles III's apartments

Halberdiers' Room

SACCHETTI ENVISAGED this as a hall for dances and festivities, with several galleries at the

▲ *René Fremin:* Philip V. *Marble and bronze. Eighteenth Century. The Landing on the Main Staircase.*

G. B. Tiepolo: Venus entrusting Vulcan with the task of forging weapons for Aeneas. *B. Rusca: Stucco decoration.* ▶
Vault in the Halberdiers' Room.

marble and painted plaster (Italian, 17th century). On them stand a beautiful model of a round temple with columns (late 18th century), from The Buen Retiro, and another in bronze of Trajan's column.

The two paintings by Luca Giordano (completed by Solimena) portraying Passages from the Life of Solomon, with others on the same subject and by the same artist, served as models for the tapestries of the King's Apartments in this New Palace, woven at the Royal Tapestry Factory under the direction of Corrado Giaquinto. From the same manufacture are the hanging with the royal coat-of-arms above the fireplace, and the covers for benches in the Chapel, all from the 18th century.

Hall of Columns

This Hall occupies the Stairwell which according to Sacchetti's project would have served as access to the Queen's Apartments. Its walls are in all details similar to those that we have ascended. The ceiling is different as it was decorated in the time of Charles III, who had the Main Staircase installed here, on the opposite side to its present position. The stuccoes were designed by Sabatini, and made by Bernardino Rusca in 1761, at the same time as those of the Halberdiers' Room; the four medallions in bas-relief depict the Four Elements. Between 1762 and the beginning of 1763, Giaquinto painted the fresco, the effect of which is therefore intended to be seen from the first flight of Sabatini's lost staircase. It should be viewed from very close to the doorway into the room, and if possible, squatting down. The subject involves an allusion to the King in the form of Apollo as a solar deity, since it represents The Sun at whose appearance all the forces of Nature become joyful and animated. Apollo,

The Hall of Columns, viewed from the Eastern wall. ▲

who advances in his chariot through the ring of the Zodiac, is accompanied by the Hours and preceded by Aurora and the Zephyr. Lower down, the seasons of the year and the elements are symbolized by Ceres, Bacchus, Venus, Vulcan, Diana, Pan and Galatea .

Also by Giaquinto, and his last work in the Palace, is The Majesty of the Crown of Spain, above the doorway we have entered. When it was painted this space was the Staircase, and this image warned visitors that they were entering the royal apartments.

From the time when Charles IV moved the ballroom here, this became the setting for Court banquets and functions that were not simply for amusement, but also ceremonial. For instance, on Maundy Thursday the King washed the feet and served the supper of twelve poor people, who symbolized the Apostles, the entire Court being present at the scene. The Washing of the Feet, a pious custom carried out by other European Monarchs besides the Spanish one –and still by the Pope today– continued to take place until the reign of Alfonso XIII. Precisely the tapestries that cover the arches illustrate The Acts of the Apostles, and they were woven in Brussels at the beginning of the 17th century from the cartoons painted by Raphael for the famous tapestries now in the Vatican. Three of the bronze sculptures are also Flemish, forming part of the series of the Seven Planets cast by Jonghellinck around 1570: The Sun, the Moon and Venus. The fourth statue is a bronze copy of the Discus Thrower, commissioned in Rome by Velázquez in 1651. The busts of Emperors in porphyry and marble are also Italian, from different periods.

The large sculpture of The Emperor Charles V dominating the Fury is a nineteenth-century copy by the Parisian bronzesmith Barbedienne (1878), of Leone Leoni's original work in the Prado Museum. Its placing here in 1879, on a neo-Plateresque pedestal, was

intended to evoke the glories of the Spanish branch of the Habsburgs, linking them with those of the Bourbons, and in this sense it should be understood as part of the reorganization of the lay-out and decoration of the Palace by Alfonso XII, who also created a room specifically intended for balls and gala banquets. For this reason, the Hall of Columns has since then been used only for the most formal events, of a ritual nature like the Washing of the Feet, or mournful such as the lying-in-state of the mortal remains of Queen Mercedes, or of a political nature like the signing of the Treaty by which Spain joined the European Community in 1985: for this act the monumental Table of the Sphinxes was used. This work, characteristic of Imperial taste after the style of Percier and Fontaine, has been attributed to the bronze craftsmanship of Thomire. Although its author may be uncertain, what we are sure of is that it was purchased by Charles IV from the widow of Godon in 1804. Its top is made of a varied sample of non-Spanish marble and hard-stone.

However, the bronze chandeliers (also Parisian, c.1846) correspond to the period when this Hall was most frequently used for festivities and balls, the reign of Queen Isabel II.

From here one continued to the Anteroom (Saleta of Charles III), in accordance with the ceremonial route in force from the time of Charles IV onwards, but nowadays the aim as far as possible is to follow the order of the King's Apartments as they were in the time of Charles III.

The ceremonial order of the rooms was governed by etiquette. Each room was destined to a particular end, while access became progressively more restricted. The origin of this type of distribution, which goes back to the beginnings of the 16th century, is a nucleus of two spaces: the Hall, for purposes of reception, and the Chamber for sleep. Thus, on

C. Giaquinto: The Sun, whose appearance brightens and enlivens all the forces of Nature.
B. Rusca: Stucco decoration. Vault in the Hall of Columns.

introducing other previous and intermediate spaces the King's Apartments sequence arises: Anteroom-Room-Saleta-Antechamber-Chamber-the private sitting room or boudoirs. The same order governed the quarters of the other Royal members of the household, but decreasing in size in accordance with their reduced rank.

The Throne Room

The Throne Room (also known as the Royal Audience Room, or the Hall of Kingdoms, or of Ambassadors) retains its entire decoration as planned and executed during the reign of Charles III, since it was totally finished by 1772. A recent restoration has returned all its splendour to this magnificent chamber, by cleaning the fresco and replacing the original velvet wall-covering with new material, transferring the original embroidery to the latter.

Here all the Sovereign's ceremonial audiences used to take place, including the last of all, as it was in this room that, according to etiquette, the mortal remains of the King lay in state prior to their removal to the Pantheon of San Lorenzo el Real. Then the tables, decorative mirrors and canopy were removed, and the draperies were changed.

Although Sacchetti had planned to cover all the walls of this gallery with marble which would have framed the mirrors and bas-reliefs nothing of this was done before the arrival of Charles III. The King decided that the decoration of this room should be directed by his man of confidence in matters of good taste Count Gazzola, who commissioned the designs for the furnishings from the Piacenza architect Giovanni Battista Natali. Apparently the choice of the painter and of the sculptor who decorated the vault may also be attributed to Gazzola.

▲ *R. Michel: Stuccowork on the vault and the lintels. G.B. Tiepolo: Fresco. A detail from the West wall of the Throne Room.*

◀ *The Throne Room, seen from the West wall.*

The magnificent effect of this union between painting, sculpture and decorative design reaches its apogee in the corners of the ceiling and the panels over the doors. The Court Sculptor Robert Michel created the ornamental stuccoes above the doorways and the cornice, with a brightness and fresh inventiveness comparable to those displayed by the great Tiepolo on the ceiling, his last masterpiece, which has always been the object of well-deserved praise even amongst his own contemporaries.

The Grandeur and Power of the Spanish Monarchy is here expressed through a large number of allegorical and allusive figures scattered over a background of open sky. When Tiepolo painted the fresco, access to the room was from the present Official Anteroom (Saleta), at that time the Antechamber to the King's Apartments (the ceiling of the Saleta was also painted by Tiepolo, with a similar subject), and the composition has to be understood by

entering from that side, opposite to where we are standing. Advancing from the door to approximately half-way along the room, the central group can be seen well: this is the Spanish Monarchy, the throne of which is set on a large globe flanked by the statues of Apollo and Minerva, surrounded by the Science of Government, Peace and Justice (near which the flying figure of Virtue is portrayed) and by Abundance and Mercy. The canopy to the throne of the Monarchy is formed by a ring of clouds surrounded by geniuses, one of whom holds the Royal Crown in the very centre of the vault. Behind this entire section of the composition, and appropriately placed adjacent to the entrance to the King's Apartments, is a pyramid or monument in honour of Charles III, with the figures of Magnanimity, Glory, Affability and Counsel. Close by are those of the three theological virtues, in addition to Prudence, Fortitude and Victory. Finally, the

G.B. Tiepolo: The Glorification of the Spanish Monarchy. *A view of the in fresco vault in the Throne Room.* ▲

Fine Arts are "depicted in one of the corners of the ceiling, showing with their attributes that they are to perpetuate the glories of the great Prince who has been their restorer", as Fabre says in his Description of the Allegories (1829).

This glorification of the Monarchy and of the Sovereign constitutes the main part of the allegory: the other half of the vault of heaven represented by the composition, the farthest from us, is inhabited by the Olympian gods. Prominent amongst them is Mercury, who as the ambassador of the gods before the Monarchy, seems to be announcing Peace on behalf of Jupiter. Apollo, sun god and protector of the Arts, is exactly over the King's throne. To the left stands Mars expelling Crime and the Furies, and opposite the throne, in a dominant position, is Neptune.

In the lowest part of the fresco, above the cornice, a numerous and varied series of characters is portrayed, possibly the most appealing part of this composition. They represent the Kingdoms of the Iberian Peninsula and the countries at that time subje to the Crown of Spain: on the side which we have entered, Andalusia, Catalonia, Aragón, Castile and Granada; on the opposite side, the East Indies, in addition to the Basque Country Cantabria, Asturias and Murcia; and on the long side over the balconies, starting from the farthest end, America with Christopher Columbus and several figures alluding to the Discovery, and then León, Galicia, Valencia and Extremadura. It is no simple matter to identify them, since Tiepolo has envisaged them with a great deal of artistic licence, in a tone of fantastic exoticism and with no preoccupation for rigour, though with grace and picturesque flair both in the whole and in the details: these include, just above the thron

▲ *G.B. Tiepolo:* Neptune in his chariot with the Nereids and other deities from Olympus, and also the allegorical figures o American viceroyalties belonging to the Spanish Crown. *A detail from the frescoes opposite the throne in the Throne Room.*

pageboy trying to catch a macaw, directly in front of the group representing America.

The remaining decoration, including the console tables, mirrors, canopy, throne and draperies, are to be understood as a whole conceived by Gazzola and the Italian artists selected by him, everything being brought from Italy, an indication of the devotion felt by Charles III for Neapolitan formulas.

The velvet was woven expressly in Genoa, thereby achieving exceptional quality, and afterwards it was sent to Naples for embroidery with gilded silver thread by the needleworker of that Court, Andrea Cottardi (or Gottard). From the various designs invited from Madrid, Paris and Naples, those selected were the ones submitted by Giovanni Battista Natali, like Gazzola a native of Piacenza, who was also responsible for designing the console tables and mirrors made by the woodcarver

Gennaro di Fiore. Between the summer of 1765 and November of the following year, all the decorative elements for this Royal Audience Chamber were made ready, though they did not occupy their intended places until 1772.

The decorative scheme designed by Natali is a key work of Italian Rococo fantasy. The characteristic themes of the late Baroque represented by Natali in the decorative carving of the twelve mirrors and matching tables, are in perfect accord with the magnificent exoticism of Tiepolo, vaguely alluding to the extensive dominions of the Spanish Monarchy: the Four Parts of the World, the Four Seasons of the Year (or the Four Periods of Life), and the Four Virtues. The whole scheme thus consists of generous rhetorical praise for the power that has there its seat.

The bronze sculptures were also placed in the Throne Room at that time, but all are of an earlier

Left. G.B. Natali: embroidery in gilded silver by A. Cottardi. A detail from the velvet tapestry in the Throne Room. ▲
Right. Jonghellinck: the god Mars, *from the* Seven Planets *series. Gilded and coated bronze. The Throne Room.*

recommendation of Sabatini. It is paradoxical that such items came to complete this Rococo setting when their style was already outmoded and only ten years before, on the instructions of Charles IV, Sabatini began to plan a new scheme of decoration for this room, radically architectural and classical, using marble and bronze with Corinthian pilasters, but this project was never carried out.

Charles IV must, however, be credited with the acquisition of three of the four splendid clocks with complex time and musical mechanisms: to the right of the canopy, a large grandfather clock with an ebony and bronze case in the Louis XVI style, made by Ferdinand Berthoud around 1780. Each of the two opposite consoles has a magnificent tabletop clock, also dating from the same period and revealing the same style. They were made in white marble and gilded bronze. One of the clocks was produced by Furet and Godon and bears the figures of Music and Astronomy. The other has allegories representing Music and was the work of 'F.L. Godon, clockmaker to His Majesty Charles'. On the left of the throne, there is another large standing clock with an ebony case and bronze rocaille. Made by John Ellicot, it displays an eighteenth-century English Georgian Style. It was a gift from the Portuguese Court on the occasion of the betrothal of Barbara of Braganza to Ferdinand VI. Ferdinand VII respected the decoration of his grandfather's time, but added the large carpet woven at the Royal Factory of Madrid which covers the geometric marquetry of coloured marble on the floor. To his reign and that of his father correspond the Empire-style candelabra on the console tables.

Finally, the feature giving its name to the room: the Throne. The original chair, of which the two seen here are faithful copies, is in the Palace of La Granja and bears the portrait of Charles III in the relief surmounting the back. Alfonso XII

date. The Four Cardinal Virtues along the wall on the throne side are usually attributed to René Frémin, as having been made for the altarpiece of the Collegiate Church at La Granja, but they have also been attributed to Foggini. Mercury, Jupiter, Saturn and Mars, with three more situated in the Hall of Columns, make up the series of the Seven Planets by Jonghellinck; the other two, a Satyr and Germanicus, are moulded from classical statues commissioned by Velázquez and made in Rome. The four bronze lions which guard the steps to the Throne are also Roman. They were made by Matteo Bonicelli in 1651 on the orders of Velázquez. Another eight lions also formed a part of this commissioned work. They were intended as decorative features for the Hall of Mirrors at the Alcazar in Madrid. These objects are now preserved as table supports in the Prado Museum.

The two chandeliers of rock crystal and silver were bought in 1780 from the Venetian Ambassador, Francesco Pesaro, on the warm

▲ *M. Bonicelli: the lions in gilded bronze (1651) which flank the flights of steps in the Throne Room.*

The Throne itself and a detail of the carpet made by the Royal Factory in the style characteristic of the reign of Ferdinand. ▲
The emblem depicting Both Worlds is symbolic of the dominions held by the Spanish Monarchy in the eighteenth century.

ordered a copy to be made of the chair, having his own profile placed in the medallion. Alfonso XIII followed suit, adding another one with Queen Victoria Eugenia's portrait in order to place them together. Similarly, the present ones carry the images of Their Majesties King Juan Carlos and Queen Sofia.

Charles III's Anteroom (Saleta)

This was the room where the King used to take his luncheon and where ordinary audiences were granted. According to the descriptions that have come down to us from travellers of the time: "His Majesty lunches alone in the room in his Apartments reserved for this purpose, and it is there, at table, that the Ministers present him with their respects. The King had scarcely started to eat, when they greeted him and withdrew, to go to the Apartments of the Prince, who was also taking luncheon. Afterwards, they returned to the King's presence, just before his table was removed. Sometimes they accompany him to his Study, remaining there with him for a quarter of an hour, and it is then that the King converses with some of them.

One gentleman places the dishes on the King's table as they are passed to him; then it is the pages who carry them. The one who presents the King with water or wine, kneels when the King begins to drink. During the meal the Nuncio remains standing a few steps in front of the table, and the King talks almost exclusively with him. When the King has finished eating, the Patriarch, who is a prelate, and therefore is dressed in the same manner as the Nuncio and the Confessor, says the prayer of thanksgiving that hardly lasts more than two or three seconds. The King crosses himself, cleans his mouth and hands, and enters his

The anteroom or 'Saleta' of Charles III, viewed from the southeast corner. ▲

allegories of Victory and her virtues are grouped on the long sides, while at the opposite end are a number of figures including the nine Muses and the Arts, around the temple of Apollo. It is a veritable discourse on the enlightened Monarch's virtues, his protection of the Arts, and so on.

The stucco designs of Sabatini were executed by Andreoli between 1761 and 1763. Also from the reign of Charles III are all the marble features and (although the present ones had not yet been installed here) the four console tables with their corresponding mirrors. From Paris are the two large chandeliers in the style of Ferdinand VII, and the circular couch, crowned by a magnificent bronze candelabrum, with bronzes by Thomire and the initials of Isabel II on the upholstery: it dates from 1846, but was not placed here until the end of the 19th century, when the long couches were also installed at the ends. The stools are from the same period. The carpet, from the Royal Factory, is dated 1880; from this period also were the silk wall-hangings, but due to their poor condition they were copied and replaced in 1994.

After Charles IV ordered the Main Staircase to be moved to its current location, this Anteroom, which formerly was entered directly from the Hall of Columns, became the first room of the King's Apartments, which extended eastwards in the opposite order to that prevailing in the time of Charles III, when it was occupied by the Prince of Asturias.

Apartments." (Moldenhawer 1782). At that time, its walls were covered during the winter with tapestries from the series of the History of Joseph, David and Salomon, woven at the Royal Tapestry Factory, under the supervision of Corrado Giaquinto, while during the summer eight large equestrian portraits were hung here, major works of Rubens and Velázquez now in the Prado Museum. But since the reign of Ferdinand VII, the pictures displayed here are four works by Luca Giordano, two on the Life of Solomon, and the other two showing scenes from Roman history, Quintus Curtius throwing himself into the Chasm and the Death of Seneca.

On the ceiling is an outstanding fresco by A.R. Mengs, The Apotheosis of Trajan (1774). This Roman Emperor, who was born in Spain and is used here as the alter ego of Charles III, is portrayed on the side opposite the entrance, seated on his throne, wearing the imperial purple and surrounded by Minerva, Hercules and Glory, who is crowning him. Different

Antechamber of Charles III (The Conversation Room)

The Antechamber or Conversation Room was where the King dined, and as such it appears (though with an idealized ceiling) in the painting by Paret of Charles III dining before his Court, which is in complete accord with the descriptions of the scene we have from the

▲ *A.R. Mengs:* Fame Proclaiming the Name of the Emperor. *A detail form the fresco entitled* The Apotheosis by Trajan. *The Vault in the 'Saleta' (anteroom) of Charles III.*

ng's contemporaries, such as Duke Fernán-
...úñez, or from French and English travellers:
...At dinner the pages bring in the different dishes
...d present them to one of the Gentlemen of the
...hamber on duty that day; he places them on
...e table; another gentleman remains standing
...ar the King to serve him wine and water,
...hich he first tastes and then presents kneeling;
...e Patriarch attends to give the blessing, and
...so, further away, are the Inquisitor General on
...e side, and the Captain of the Guard on the
...her. The Ambassadors form a circle around
...d converse with the King for a moment when
...ey withdraw with him to the neighbouring
...om, which is entered by the door behind his
...air. The rest of the Court forms a second outer
...rcle. When the King rises from the table, all

those to be presented to him come forward, and
if the Corregidor of Madrid receives an
appropriate indication he enters with the
Ambassadors into the Chamber. The King goes
out to take exercise every day of the year, even
in rain or storm, though if in Madrid he only
does so in the afternoon, but if he is in the
country, at one of the Seats, he goes out morning
and afternoon." (William Darlymperle, 1774).

The tapestries that decorated this room in
the time of Charles III were those of the *History
of Joseph*, made at the Royal Factory from
cartoons painted in 1770 by José del Castillo,
under the direction of Giaquinto. During the
summer masterpieces by Titian, Van Dyck and
Velázquez, including The Meninas, used to
hang here. Originally intended for this room

L. Paret y Alcázar: Charles III dining before the Court. *Eighteenth Century. The Prado Museum.* ▲

as patron of the Arts, to which the beautiful group of Apollo and the Muses above the entrance door refers. The restrained decorative stuccoes, made by Bernardino Rusca, were also designed by the painter and not by Sabatini. The latter yielded to his friend Mengs after confronting Giaquinto, who was initially to have decorated this ceiling. The incident with his two rivals, who were favoured by the King, led the painter of Ferdinand VI to decide to leave Spain by now old and infirm. The four oval reliefs in the corners are by Felipe de Castro.

The canvases, masterpieces by Goya, are two pairs of portraits of Charles IV and his wife Queen María Luisa of Parma: one set is more formal, showing the King wearing the uniform of Colonel of the Life Guards and the Queen in Court dress, while the other is more casual, with the King wearing hunting attire and the Queen dressed as a Spanish "maja", with a black skirt and mantilla. These are the most outstanding paintings to be seen today in the Palace, and the first pair have been in this room since the reign of Ferdinand VII. As a counterpoint to Goya's works, we have two marble busts of the same royal couple, by Juan Adán (1797).

Also from the reign of Charles IV are the console tables, the stools, and the magnificent clock in the shape of a small temple. It is made of mahogany, bronze and porcelain. The base of the clock holds a flute organ. Within the temple, there are white marble sculptures depicting Chronos holding up the celestial sphere. On top of the clock, charity is portrayed in porcelain. The design is attributed to J.D. Dugourc. It was the last work (1799) of the clockmaker Louis Godon, a distinguished supplier of Parisian decorative objects to Charles IV. The continuation of this style in the first three decades of the nineteenth century, during the reign of Ferdinand VII, can be seen in the armchairs and in the great circular bronze and mahogany divan.

were the magnificent console tables of hard-stones and bronze, masterpieces of the Royal Factory of The Buen Retiro, which are also to be found in the Prado Museum at present.

The marble decoration from the reign of Charles III has survived, and from the same period is the very good fireplace which, unusually, still retains its bronzes. However, painting, both of the ceiling and on canvas, is the absolute protagonist of this room.

The fresco by Anton Raphael Mengs depicts The Apotheosis of Hercules. The hero, traditionally used in Spain as the personification or emblem of the King, is welcomed among the gods on Mount Olympus as a reward for his great feats: the aim is to praise Charles III as an illustrious military and political figure, as well

▲ *F. de Goya:* Queen Maria Luisa of Parma in Court Costume. *The Antechamber of Charles III.*

The Antechamber of Charles III, viewed from the northeast corner.

The Chamber was where the King dressed and received private audiences. Therefore, we should not be surprised at the excellence with which Charles III wished it to be decorated, entrusting the design of each and every element to his Royal Painter Mattia Gasparini, whom he had brought with him from Naples. It is logical that the artist's name has served to identify this room of the Palace since the time of Ferdinand VII, inasmuch as the marble floor, the stucco ceiling, the silk wall-hangings embroidered with gold and silver thread, the furniture of precious woods and bronzes, were all entirely designed by Gasparini, who until his death directed this supreme work of the Barochetto. After his death it was continued under the supervision of his widow and son, and of his successor in the post of Chamber Decorator, G.B. Ferroni.

Made by Italian craftsmen and German cabinetmakers, this room can claim to be of Madrid only insofar as it was commissioned in this city by one who had previously been King of Naples, and in reality it is an international work, one of the most perfect examples of the European late Baroque. The Rococo decoration based on asymetrical vegetation shines forth in its maximum splendour, heavy with exotic fantasy of Chinese inspiration. One cannot but admire its magnificence, though to find the taste for it and to lose oneself happily amongst its rich arabesques it is necessary to forget Goya and Mengs, escaping into the dream world also suggested by the Throne Room.

This decorative scheme is preserved intact, and indeed, more complete than when its creator and the Monarch who commissioned it were able to contemplate it, since such extensive work took many years to complete. As the embroidered wall-hangings were not finished until 1802, fourteen years after the death of Charles III, during his reign in wintertime the walls were hung with tapestries made by the Royal Factory, from cartoons by Antonio Gónzalez Velázquez in the style of David Teniers, of whom the King was so fond. In summertime, paintings by Diego Velázquez were hung here, including Vulcan's Forge, The Tapestry Weavers and The Tipplers, in addition to works by Murillo, Ribera and Titian. Since the King greatly admired Mengs, this artist's last work, The Annunciation, was also displayed here; it is now in the Royal Chapel.

The Shepherd's Clock above the fireplace is a masterpiece by Jacquet Droz, given both its fine case in the Louis XV style and its complex mechanism with music and automata. It was acquired by Ferdinand VI in 1758. The other clock is also the work of Droz. Its attractive case, in the same style, stands on the console table between the two balconies.

The embroidered wall-hangings were not installed until 1815. Alfonso XII had them restored in 1879, and since then the curtains, which are also embroidered and used to cover the doors and windows, are in storage. In the last great restoration campaign the embroidery was transferred onto a new silk background.

With the exception of the superb set of chairs of fine woods and bronze, none of the furniture corresponds to Gasparini's scheme. From the time of Charles IV are the exellent console tables, with bronzes by Domingo Urquiza and work by the cabinetmakers of the Royal Workshops, as well as the French candelabra, including outstanding examples of the "Etruscan" taste in porcelain and bronze. The splendid chandelier has the greatest symbolic meaning of the many such pieces commissioned by Ferdinand VII, displaying his monogram and that of his third wife María Josefa Amalia of Saxony. The table corresponds to the period of Isabel II: it was designed and made in Rome by

erardo Volponi and Guglielmo Chidel, under the direction of Filippo Agricola in 1848.

Three adjoining small rooms which are not sited were the offices of Charles III, the -called Rooms of Woods from the Indies, due the rich decoration also designed by asparini, which subsequently was dismantled nd installed in other rooms of the Palace. rdinand VII, who also had his study or small rivate room in this suite, commissioned the iling frescoes by Luis López.

ne "Tramcar" of Charles III

his room was given its present layout in 1880, hen an attempt was made to improve the ow between the Gasparini Room and the new nqueting Hall; its name also dates from that time, alluding to its long, narrow shape. Until then there had been two rooms here: one was used only as a passageway, as it is nowadays, being very small but literally covered by pictures during the reigns of Charles III and Charles IV, and overfilled with furniture in that of Isabel II; the other interior room was larger, and served as the Oratory of Charles III, with access from the Chamber. It was designed by Sabatini, the walls being adorned with green Lanjarón marble and engraved gilded bronzes made in 1767-1768 by Urquiza, Vendetti and Beya: the ceiling with stuccoes, was by Bernardino Rusca; over the High Altar was a fresco by Mengs, The Adoration of the Shepherds. Other similar oratories, designed and built by Sabatini with a similar degree of magnificence, were also dismantled at the end of the 19th century. These spaces, destined for

M. Gasparini: Fine-wood chairs, bronze statues and embroidered silk tapestry, created by German and Italian artisans. ▲
The Royal Chamber of Charles III.

morning and evening devotions, were important in the daily life of the Royal Family.

Now there are two console tables here, dating back to around 1780, the design of which is ascribed to Sabatini; two portraits, Francis of Portugal attributed to Ranc, and James (III) Stuart, The Old Pretender to the English Throne, attributed to Francisco Trevisani; and a tapestry cartoon, The Wild-Boar Hunt by José del Castillo. In the restoration campaign of 1991 new fabric was installed on the walls of this room; it was specially made with the ciphers of King Juan Carlos and Queen Sofía.

Charles III's Hall

The first plans for the distribution of the royal apartments designated this as a bedroom, and so it was for Charles III, from 1764 until the 13th of December 1788, when he died here. Nothing remains of the original furniture, which was selected by Sabatini, and included outstanding tapestries, carved and gilded chairs by Chiani and Balce, and the splendid fireplace bronzes of Vendetti. The paintings, on the Passion of Christ, were all by Mengs: four above the doorways, and a large Descent from the Cross by Mariano Salvador Maella, where now hangs the portrait of Charles III, this Monarch of the Enlightenment being portrayed in the ceremonial habit of the honorary Order that he founded to reward merit; he had named it after himself, placing it under the patronage of the Immaculate Conception of the Virgin, for whom he felt a particular devotion. The present aspect of this room is that of a sanctuary, dedicated to Charles III and to his Order by his grandson Ferdinand VII, as expressed by the Latin inscription on the ceiling: "To Charles III, a deeply religious Monarch, instituting the Spanish Order under the protection of the

Immaculate Virgin / To reward virtue and me / On the very ceiling beneath which he passed on to a better life and to receive a greater heavenly recompense for his virtue and his merit / His grandson Ferdinand VII wished th to be painted in the year 1828". Ferdinand VII, who had also been using this Room as a bedroom when he was Prince of Asturias, turned it into his Dressing Room after he became King.

The furniture of white and gilded wood is typical of the Ferdinand VII style. The new, elegant neo-classical fireplace in the Ionic order, in white, pink and green marble, seems to be Italian. The blue grogram wall-hangings with superimposed white embroidered motifs alluding to the Order, are also in the Ferdinand VII style: stripes, stars, castles, lion and ciphers of Charles III; they are original, except for the blue silk background which has twice been replaced, the first time during the reign of Alfonso XII, and the second during th 1986 restoration.

In addition to the overall effect, the most remarkable aspect of this decorative scheme is the fresco painting on the ceiling, where Vicente López portrayed The Institution of the Order of Charles III: the King, in gala uniform and with all the emblems of sovereignty, is kneeling before the Immaculate Virgin. Near the altar are figures representing Religion, Piety, Gratitude, the Spanish Monarchy, Publi Happiness and Pleasure. Above the south wa over the fireplace, are Nobility, Honour, Merit and Virtue; while above the opposite wall is a allegory of the Benefits of Peace, accompanied by "Noble Agriculture" and children throwing weapons into a blazing abyss, where the dragon of Discord is also to be seen, while Evi and Rebellion are fleeing. Over the balconies, History, Time and Fame. The stucco decoratio on the cornice is by José Tomás and José Giné:

The Hall of Charles III, viewed from the southwest corner.

◀ *The Royal Chamber of Charles III or the Gasparini Room, seen from the southwest corner.*

completing that of the fresco: at the corners, sustained by geniuses are four emblems alluding to the King; and in the central section three reliefs on the foundation of the Order and its aims.

Ferdinand VII kept the pictures of Mengs in their original places, and he decorated this Dressing Room with furniture that is no longer here, since under Alfonso XIII the console tables and the Ferdinand VII mirrors were replaced by the present ones, which are in the Rococo style and therefore earlier. Of the immense profusion of decorative bronze objects that were once here, two extraordinary pieces have been retained in their places: the chandelier in the shape of a fleur-de-lys, heraldic symbol of the Bourbon Dynasty, purchased in Paris around 1825 for this room by order of Ferdinand VII; and the amphora clock (c. 1800), of gilded and blued bronze, with clock and automatons by J.F. De Belle, also from Paris.

Although it was not placed here until the reign of Isabel II (who otherwise fully respected the Ferdinand VII- style decoration of this Room), the sumptuous Pedestal Table of the Coronation of Charles X (1825), in bronze and Sèvres porcelain, a gift from the French Monarch to his Spanish counterpart, also dates back to the reign of Ferdinand VII.

Porcelain Room

Encouraged by his wife, María Amalia of Saxony, Charles VI of the Two Sicilies had created the famous Capodimonte Porcelain Factory near Naples. After inheriting the Spanish Throne as Charles III, in 1760 he gave orders that the workers and the materials be taken to Madrid, thus establishing the Royal Factory of The Buen Retiro. He wished to have in his Spanish palaces a porcelain room like that of the Porticci Palace, and he commenced with the one in Aranjuez. Only when it was completed, by 1765, was the preparation of another "China Room" begun for the Palace of Madrid, the installation being completed in 177 The porcelain work is by the same team, directed by Giuseppe Gricci, but attention has always been drawn to the drastic change in tast to be observed between the two rooms: as against the Chinese shapes and themes of Aranjuez, directly linked to the Porticci room designed by Natali, the one in Madrid adopts classical late-Baroque forms, which, in general, have been less appreciated than the unrestraine Rococo of the other room. The design is close to the taste of Ferroni, but the author is unknown. Names invoked have included the painters Juar Bautista de la Torre and Jenaro Boltri, employee of the Factory. The walls and the ceilings were covered with frames to hold the porcelain pane made up of numerous interconnected layers decorated by corbels, urns and white and gold medallions with floral motifs and vines in gree shades. This whole setting contains allegories o the Dionysius festivals. The splendid porcelain and bronze vases also come from the Buen Retiro, but are of a very different taste from tha of the walls, since they date from the reign of Charles IV, like the console tables of carved and painted wood on which they stand, and the planetary-clock by Breguet, in the shape of a sphere supported by the Titan Atlas in the cent of the room.

Yellow Room

This room owes its name, and that of Room o the Crowns by which it was known in the 19th century, to the wall-hangings installed here or the instructions of Ferdinand VII; the walls are now covered by several p anels of fabric wove

The Porcelain Room.

at the Royal Factory from cartoons by José del Castillo under the direction of Francesco Sabatini, for the Bedroom of Charles III. In addition to covering the walls, curtains for doors and balconies were also included, with coverings for the bed and bedspread, the chairs and other pieces of furniture, as well as for both sides of the fireplace screen, that here take the place of pelmets. The yellow silk framing the fabric panels was renewed in 1995.

At the beginning of the reign of Charles III, this room was intended to be the Queen's Private Sitting Room, suggested by the topic of the fresco painted by Gian Domenico Tiepolo, Juno in her Chariot. From 1766 onwards, it was at the service of Charles III, who filled it with paintings by Teniers and Breughel, and excellent small portraits by Van Dyck and Velázquez. Remaining from that period is the socle of fine-wood marquetry made by German cabinetmakers from the workshop directed by Gasparini.

Ferdinand VII installed his bedroom here. He ordered Tiepolo's fresco to be erased, and Luis López to paint a new one, the theme of which is related to the new use of the room: *Juno, on her golden chariot drawn by peacocks, and accompanied by Hymen, moves towards the place where Morpheus is sleeping.*

The French furniture brought together here is the most outstanding of its type in the Palace. It was designed by Jean-Démosthène Dugourc, an important decorator who worked a great deal for Charles IV, first in France and later in Madrid, making items that mark the transition between the Louis XVI taste and the Empire style. Still within the former category are the chest-of-drawers and the secrétaire made around 1790 by Forestier and Gouthière. The remaining pieces of furniture are characteristic of the "Etruscan style", in which Dugourc was a pioneer, a precursor of the Empire style. The sumptuous pedestal table, inspired by pieces of furniture found at Pompeii and Herculaneum, supports a horizontal spherical clock made by Godon. It forms a part of the panel and has five concentric circles indicating hours, months, the signs of the Zodiac, calendar and weekly periods. The six chairs also follow archaeological models that are not in any way Spanish, despite the similarity of their back design to an ornamental hair-comb; they belong to a set made for the apartments of Queen María Luisa in the Palace of Aranjuez. Also dating to around 1800, but from Madrid, are the carpet from the Royal Factory, the two Buen Retiro vases, and the clock on the bureau, signed by Manuel Gutiérrez. The lamp is in the Ferdinand VII style (though it is not the one that was here at that time), as are the candelabra; the wall lamps date from the reign of Isabel II, when the King Consort, Francisco de Asís, had his

J.D. Dugourc: Secrétaire, made by Forestier and Gouthière, C. 1790. Mahogany palm, with engraved and gilded bronzes. The Yellow Room.

The Yellow Room.

Dressing Room here. From the time of Alfonso XII onwards, it has served as a Sitting-Room and leads on to the Banqueting Hall.

The Queen's Apartments: The Banqueting Hall and adjacent rooms

The Banqueting Hall

THE LENGTH of the great hall for balls and gala dinners is striking, since it is the result of joining together the three central rooms on the western façade. These rooms, and the three corresponding interior ones looking towards the main courtyard through the Gallery, during the reign of Charles III formed the Queen's apartments, intended for the Monarch's spouse who never occupied them since she died in 1760 before the Palace was in a habitable condition, but in fact used by the Queen Mother Isabella Farnese. The rooms facing onto the galleries served as antechambers. The last of these led to the Room for Luncheons and Audiences, corresponding to the most distant section from the entrance door; the central area was the Chamber, and the closest one to the King's quarters was the Bedroom, a logical arrangement allowing private passage between the apartments of the royal spouses.

Later occupied by the Infanta María Josefa and by the Princess of Asturias, this room was used again by the Queen during the reign of Ferdinand VII, who ordered important rehabilitation and redecoration work to be undertaken. Under Isabel II it was occupied by the King Consort Francisco de Asís, but when after the First Republic the Restoration returned the throne to the Bourbons, Alfonso XII wanted, instead of so many sets of apartments with large and medium-sized rooms and small studies, to have a large hall where gala banquets for more

The Banqueting Hall, seen from the northern wall.

including the fifteen chandeliers and the ten wall lamps. Also from Paris are the chairs for a maximum number of one hundred and forty-four persons. The table has never been anything more than a frame without value as a piece of furniture, and it can be taken to pieces so that the room can also be used for balls.

For the decoration of the walls, the solution adopted was very much in line with the historicist taste of the epoch, the free spaces being covered with tapestries from the Royal Collection, forming part of the Vertumnus and Pomona series, woven at the end of the 16th century in Brussels by Pannemaker, from cartoons by Vermeyer. The decoration of this room of King Alfonso XII is completed with twelve large 18th-century Chinese jars, and several large French 19th-century vases of gilded bronze and Sèvres porcelain, placed in the balcony recesses: six make up a series of historic scenes relating to the Kings of France and Spain, painted by Lachassagne and Renaud (1830), and the other two (beside the first and last balconies) have landscapes, from the middle of the century.

To conclude, it is worthwhile to examine the frescoes painted to decorate the Queen's Apartments before the Dining Room was created In the first section, where the bedroom used to be, the fresco is by Mengs, portraying Aurora. In 1880, the original stuccoes and other scenes by the same artist also on the ceiling were destroyed (they represented The Four Moments of the Day around the central scene), because for the sake of symmetry Sabatini's stucco decoration was copied, as it appears on the ceiling at the other end of the Dining Room. Another feature that disappeared was the frieze painted in the upper section of the walls by Langlois and Alejandro González Velázquez. Ferdinand VII had it decorated ostentatiously in the "Turkish manner" as a "Grand Private Sitting Room of the Queen", with rich green damask draperies.

than one hundred people could be served. Therefore, in 1879 he commissioned his architect José Segundo de Lema to join these three rooms together, supporting the transversal walls on lowered arches with matching columns, in such a way that both the structure and the decoration of the ceilings would remain intact. The work was not finished until 1885.

The architect succeeded in giving coherence to a space clearly sectioned into three parts and where the decoration of the ceilings is 18th-century, while on the walls the influence of the contemporary French neo-Baroque taste is evident in both the design, in which details of different origins (mainly Louis XVI) are brought together, and in the materials, since the columns are of Bagnères marble and most of the bronze work was executed in Paris,

▲ The Phoenix Jar. *China in the Chi'ien-lung era (1736-1795) during the Ch'ing dynasty (1644-1912). The Banqueting Hall.*

The fresco on the central vault corresponding to the Queen's Chamber, is by Antonio González Velázquez, and depicts Columbus offering the New World to the Catholic Monarchs, with four chiaroscuro medallions representing Mexico, Peru, Chile and the Philippine Islands. In 1818 Ferdinand VII decided on a great decorative scheme aimed at turning this room into the "Grand Boudoir" of the new Queen, his second wife María Isabel of Braganza: the fundamental pieces, besides the remarkable Empire-style furniture and the sumptuous orange silk drapery, were the six chiaroscuro paintings above the doorways, one of them by Goya, two by Vicente López and the other three by Zacarías G. Velázquez, Aparicio and Camarón. The presence of a work by Goya and the overall sense of unity gave this room an extraordinary importance.

The fresco on the last vault is by Francisco Bayeu; this was the third antechamber or Luncheon and Royal Audience Room of the Queen, and the fresco represents Boabdil delivering the Keys of Granada to the Catholic Monarchs. It is interesting that, in contrast to the mythological and allegorical themes dominating the other ceiling frescoes of the Palace, historical topics were chosen for the Queen's Apartments, turning to the figure of Isabel the Catholic, in two of her most outstanding moments, as a reference point and inevitable model for any Spanish Sovereign. During the reign of Ferdinand VII this room was known as the Queen's Oratory, and under Isabel II, when it fulfilled the same role for the King Consort, the large circular couch with bronzes by Thomire which is now in the Saleta of Charles III was here.

F. Bayeu: Boabdil Surrendering the Keys of Granada to the Catholic Monarchs. *A detail from the fresco on the northern wall of the Banqueting Hall.* ▲

Antechamber or Plateresque Room

Under Charles III this was the first of the Queen's Antechambers. When the Banqueting Hall was created, Lema also modified the three rooms located between it and the Main Gallery, in order to use them as relief, service and transit areas: he demolished all the partitions and ceilings that had divided it into smaller rooms during the reigns of Charles III and Charles IV, returning them to their original sizes, and he decorated the central one with pilasters and other architectural elements with motifs from the Spanish "plateresque" style, carved in wood by Manuel Genné. Within the taste for using historical styles, this decoration is curious for such an early use of this national Renaissance repertoire rather than the Italian forms of the Quattrocento. The intention had

been to gild the relief of the carving to make it stand out more, but finally everything remained white, though beside a door a sample was left to show how the room would have looked with the use of varnish and gilding for the carving. This sudden interruption is explained by the death of Alfonso XII in 1885.

During the reign of Alfonso XIII, it began to be called the Cinema Room because it was used to project films for the Royal Family although it was also named the Band Room as it held the music band of the Royal Guard when they provided entertainment for grand banquets in the adjoining Banqueting Hall. Currently on display is an important centrepiece or 'dessert' in gilded bronze, hard stones and enamels. It was made by Luigi Valadier in Rome in 1778 and was immediately bought by the 'Baily' of the order of Malta, Jacques-Laure de Breteuil;

▲ *The Roman Workshop of L. Valadier and of Hard Stones from the Royal Factory of the Buen Retiro, Madrid. The Dessert of Prince Carlos (Charles IV), 1778-1789. Hard Stones, engraved and gilded bronzes, and enamels. The Plateresque Room.*

llowing his death, it was acquired in a Paris uction in 1786 by the Count of Aranda for the rince of Austrias. When the Prince had become harles IV, the centrepiece was extended in the lard Stone workshop at the Royal Factory of he Buen Retiro.

Along the walls, six display cabinets are ositioned at regular intervals. They hold a election of important medals minted from the me of Philip V to the present day. These edals belong to the collection kept at the oyal Library.

ntechamber or Silverware Room

his was the second of the Queen's ntechambers; as in the preceding and following nes, the alterations of Charles IV and Ferdinand VII led to the loss of the ceiling fresco, and in 1880 Lema also restored its original dimensions: it was he who installed here the elegant wood and marble socle. Currently, a selection of the domestic silverware used by the Royal Family is exhibited here. Unfortunately, Joseph Bonaparte ordered all the older pieces to be melted down in order to support the cost of the war, and so the very rich eighteenth-century royal silverware was lost. Those items now on show are from the 19th century.

They include some made in the Martínez Silver Factory of Madrid, commissioned by Ferdinand VII for the Boudoir of Queen María Isabel of Braganza, in addition to many other pieces from the reigns of Isabel II and Alfonso XII and XIII. A detailed explanation is not given here because descriptions are provided in the show-cases, and because they are regularly transferred

The Madrid Workshop (attributed to José or Baltasar Salazar): A tray 1747-1755. Gilded Silver embossed with rocaille. ▲
The Silver Room.

this room had a ceiling fresco, The Power of Spain in the Four Parts of the World, ascribed by Fabre to Luis González Velázquez. During the reign of Alfonso XII it was the Saleta of the Infanta Isabel, from which time dates the present rather dull ceiling painting by the stage-set designers Busato and Bonardi.

Antechamber or Stradivarius Room

Here are exhibited the quartet of instruments (viola, violoncello and two violins) made for the King of Spain by the celebrated Cremona luthier Antonio Stradivari, and finally acquired by Charles IV, and another violoncello by the same craftsman.

The ceiling retains the decoration of stucco and painting dating back to the reign of Charles III; the fresco portrays Benignity accompanied by the Four Cardinal Virtues, and it is the work of one of the González Velázquez brothers (Antonio according to Ponz and Ceán, or his brother Luis according to Fabre), Giaquinto's disciples. In those days this room was used for Luncheons and Audiences by the Infante Luis, and from 1785 onwards by the Infante Gabriel, who placed here the best pictures in his collection. Under Ferdinand VII it was the Queen's dining room, and later on the antechamber of Montpensier and the Infanta Isabel. The paving, consisting of colourful marble marquetry, is from the time of Charles III. It originates from the adjoining third Antechamber of the Queen. In 1880, this room became a part of the Banqueting Hall.

Chamber of the Infante Don Luis or The Musical Instruments Room

The ceiling is admirably painted in fresco by Francisco Bayeu, who comes close to the quality

to other places. The religious silverware is in the Reliquary and in the adjacent strong-room of the Royal Chapel, and is not seen at the present time.

Apartments of the Infante Luis

THE NEXT three rooms visited were the first ones of the Suite occupied from 1764 until his exile from the Court by the Infante Luis, brother of Charles III, and from 1785 onwards by the Infante Gabriel. In the reign of Isabel II they were assigned to the Duke and Duchess of Montpensier, and in the time of Alfonso XII and Alfonso XIII to the Infanta Isabel, known as "la Chata" (the snub-nosed).

In the First Antechamber, through which we pass but which we will see again on leaving, a selection of royal porcelain tableware is exhibited. Before the changes introduced by Ferdinand VII,

▲ *The Royal Factory of Martínez Silverware: A large jug from the Boudoir of Queen María Isabel de Braganza, 1815. Engraved and Gilded Silver. The Silver Room.*

p. A. González Velázquez: Gentleness accompanied by the Four Cardinal Virtues. *Fresco on the vault of the Stradivarius Room.* ▲
Below. A. Stradivarius: Palace Quartet, cello, viola and two violins. *The Stradivarius Room.*

of his master Mengs in this work, Providence presiding over the Virtues and Faculties of Man, the best of those that he undertook in the Palace. The wallpaper is new, but resembles a model from the reign of Ferdinand VII.

Several musical instruments from the 18th and 19th centuries are exhibited here, including the outstanding upright pianos shaped in imitation of bookshelves, built for Charles IV by Francisco Fernández (1805) and Francisco Flórez (1807); the one by Flórez is exquisitely decorated with bronzes, fine woods and painted crystal. Two pianos for children, one of them by Lesieur and the other by Rodrigo Ten (1918); some early nineteenth-century guitars; and two harps by Erard (1861). The Italian stipo follows the Florentine models typical of

the 17th century, but it appears to be Milanese from the 19th century.

The equestrian statue of Louis XV is positioned on the table in the centre which is from the reign of Ferdinand VII. The statue originated from the collection owned by the Count of Paroy and was later acquired by Charles IV. It is a smaller eighteenth-century model of the original made by Bouchardon for the Louis XV Square in Paris. The statue was knocked down and destroyed during the French Revolution. It was replaced by the guillotine which ended the life of Louis XVI. Subsequently, Louis XVIII ordered that the Egyptian obelisk from the Temple of Luxor be put in its place. Since then, this is the monument that has presided over Concorde Square.

▲ *F. Bayeu:* Providence Presiding over the Virtues and Faculties of Man. *A detail from the fresco on the vault of the Chamber of the Infante Luis.*

Antechamber or Chinaware Room

The other rooms in these apartments –the Dressing Room, the Bedroom, the Angled Room, and the Bird Room– were occupied first by the Infante Luis and then by the Infante Gabriel during the reign of Charles III. The balconies face the Park and the Gardens. Although the rooms are small, they hold a selection of the most important works from the Collection of Painting belonging to Patrimonio Nacional (National Heritage), including pictures by Juan de Flandes y Zitow, Van der Weyden, Cossiers, Caravaggio, Jusepe Leonardo, Bayeu, Maella, Velazquez, Goya and Mengs. The display also contains ceilings painted in fresco in the eighteenth century by González, Velazquez, Maella, Lorenzo and Gian Domenico Tiepolo. It also includes the only surviving original wallpaper in the palace from the reign of Ferdinand VII. Currently, these rooms are not open to the public.

Returning to this antechamber we can contemplate a selection from the most important services of tableware which can be admired in this room: one belonging to Philip V, of East India Company porcelain; one of Charles III, commissioned from Meissen in 1738; and the one of the Prince and Princess of Asturias, Charles and María Luisa, made at Sèvres in 1776. Some consolation for the loss of so many of the eighteenth-century pieces is the abundance of those ordered from Paris by Ferdinand VII and Isabel II, especially the so-called Landscape set from the Parisian manufacturers Boin au Palais Royal.

The Gallery and the Main Courtyard

THE SPACIOUS corridor surrounding the courtyard at the level of the main floor allowed entry into the suites of each royal personage by way of their respective guard room or antechamber, thus being the main artery for the

Left. The Indies Company: Sugar bowl from the Chinaware of Philip V. From the first third of the eighteenth century. ▲
The Chinaware Room. Right. Boin au Palais Royal, Paris: a dish with a View of Burgos, from the Landscape Chinaware,
c. 1828. The Chinaware Room.

circulation of the courtiers. It was also accessible from the two general staircases communicating with the upper floors, known as the Cáceres and Ladies' Staircases, which are located in the northwest and northeast corners.

The architecture of the Gallery is as it was conceived by Sacchetti, except that in his project the large windows would have been divided by stone jambs and lintels. Charles III ordered Sabatini to close them simply with large iron frames, as we see them now. He further gave instructions that the series of reliefs on political, military, scientific and religious subjects which Father Sarmiento had intended to place in panels above the windows, should not be installed; those that were made are now in the Prado Museum or the Academy of San Fernando.

Through any of the large windows one may contemplate the noble architecture of the Courtyard, which is square, and slightly displaced to the North within the square shape of the Palace, since from the outset the architect had planned the southern range to be wider in order to accomodate the Main Staircase and the Chapel (which in the old Alcázar lay between the two Courtyards of the King and the Queen). In order to emphasize the axis of the main entrance, Sacchetti made the central arches of the south and north sides wider, at the expense of narrowing the side arches, where are seen the four statues of Roman emperors that Charles III had removed from below the large balcony on the façade; Sabatini placed them here in 1791.

For great ceremonies the Gallery was carpeted and the walls were covered with

▲ *Right. The Main Gallery. Left. G.D. Olivieri:* The Emperor Honorio, *c. 1760. Colmenar Stone. The Main Courtyard.*

pestries from the Royal Collection, so that the
pproach to the Chapel appeared more
mpressive.

he Royal Chapel

HE DOOR of the Royal Chapel opens out onto
he Gallery. Here, two vaulted niches stand
ver the entrance. They contain sculptures of
he Catholic Monarchs. The sculptures were
arved by Jose Vilches as commissioned work
n Rome in 1862.

Both the sculptures of The Catholic Monarchs
anking the doorway to The Royal Chapel are
he work of Ponciano Ponzano. In 1742, due to
riticism by Scotti, it was decided not to locate
he Chapel as originally intended, where the

Halberdiers' Room is now situated, but on its
current site, by eliminating several of the rooms
planned for the Infantes. After putting forward
several options, always aimed at increasing the
size of the Chapel, Sacchetti formulated his
definitive plan in 1748, following which it was
built exactly as it is today. Nevertheless, the
decoration was never completed according to
the ideas of the architect, who had planned for
the floors and all the walls to be of marble, and
for the capitals and bases of the columns and
pilasters to be of bronze. Moreover, neither the
altarpieces, nor the form of the Screen (enclosing
the glazed gallery at the west end of the Chapel,
destined for use by the Monarchs) and the
Choir, follow Sacchetti's final proposal.
Charles III ordered the Chapel to be completed
"provisionally" in stucco, as it appears

nowadays, since he planned to extend it by adding a projection towards the north, for which Sabatini prepared two projects that were fortunately never put into effect.

The decoration proposed by Sacchetti, with the collaboration of Ventura Rodríguez and Corrado Giaquinto, if it ever had been completed, would have achieved a magnificence difficult to equal. Of this scheme, what was carried out is the whole decoration of the ceilings, and the ten large columns made from single pieces of black marble from Mañaria (Basque Country).

From the cornice upwards, everything is by Giaquinto: his are the designs of the stuccoes, painted by Andreoli, and again his are the grandiose frescoes representing St.James at Clavijo above the entrance doorway, Glory, with the Holy Trinity Crowning the Virgin in the dome, and in the pendentives Saints Leandro, Dámaso, Isidoro, Hermenegildo, Isidro Labrador and María de la Cabeza; The Holy Trinity in the Gallery behind the High Altar –because it was originally intended to place them further back in the apse– and in the Choir, the Allegory of Religion. The Stucco Angels are by Felipe de Castro, except for the ones flanking the eucharistic symbol on the High Altar arch. The latter were made by Olivieri.

In comparison to the sumptuous effect of the vaults, the picture over the High Altar is very modest: St. Michael by Ramón Bayeu after a lost original by Giordano and a drawing by his master Mengs. Precisely Mengs was responsible for the Annunciation, his last work, left unfinished at his death in Rome in 1779. The architecture of both altarpieces is by Sabatini, except for the table of the Annunciation, by Isidro Velázquez, containing the relics of the Roman martyr St. Felix. The neo-classical sculptures of The Four Evangelists are from the reign of Ferdinand VII. They were produced by

José Ginés and are located in the Ante-Chapel. Also from this period are the sculptures of lampadary angels by Esteban de Agreda. They are situated in the chancel. Subsequently, Isabel II commissioned Juan Samsó with the task of creating the sculptures of the Sacred Hearts which flank the Annunciation Altar.

In addition to the daily worship conducted by a numerous body of Chaplains, at whose head was the Cardinal Patriarch of the Indies, His Majesty's Almoner and Principal Chaplain, the solemn ceremonies were undertaken with great pomp. Usually, the King and other members of the Royal Family would follow the service from the screen or glazed gallery at the west end of the Chapel reached from the interior of the royal apartments, but on solemn feast days the Sovereign would come out in procession by way of the Gallery around the Courtyard decked out with tapestries. On reaching the Chapel he would bow before the altar, and then again before the Queen who was standing at the Screen, then occupying his seat of honour beneath the canopy. Every member of the Court had a place assigned: directly beside the King were the Chamberlain of the Palace and the Captain of the Royal Guard, then the Grandees facing the door, and so on. The public was only allowed to occupy the entrance section, or Ante-Chapel.

Ferdinand VI wished for a sumptuous though not particularly large Chapel, and so he aimed at splendour in all the details, including the numerous liturgical vestments (particularly the cope bearing his name), the choir books and the organ, since music was of great importance to this Monarch, as it had been to his father, and the Royal Chapel had a numerous yet select group of instrumentalists and singers. The organ, with a case designed by Ventura Rodríguez, was begun by Leonardo Fernández Dávila and finished by Jorge Bosch, from Mallorca. It is unique in Spain due not only to

its intrinsic quality, but also because it escaped any modification in the nineteenth century. It has recently been scrupulously restored.

The Guard Room and back-rooms of Queen María Luisa

Guard Room of Queen Maria Luisa

THIS ROOM provided access from the Gallery to the Apartments of the Princess, and later Queen, María Luisa. They are not open to visitors at present. The balconies of these apartments open onto the East Square. Subsequently, it was the Anteroom of the Apartments of Queen María Luisa of Habsburg. The simplicity which its original use imposed on this room is quite at

odds with the present decoration, which is dominated by ostentatious pieces from the reign of Ferdinand VII, such as, the round table in bronze and malachite by Guillermo Déniere, with a small temple dedicated to Apollo and the Muses, and the marble dessert or table-centre. There are portraits of five 19th century European monarchs hanging in this room: between the windows, María Amalia of Saxony, Queen of Spain and the third wife of Ferdinand VII, by Vicente López; the latter also painted the portrait of Francis I of the Two Sicilies, which is hanging on the back wall. We have Louis Philippe of Orleans and Maria Amalia of the Two Sicilies, the French monarchs painted by Winterhalter, on each side of the fireplace. Alfonso XII, by Federico de Madrazo faces them. The two late 17th century baroque paintings hanging on either

▲ *C. Giaquinto:* The Glory, with the Holy Trinity crowning the Virgin. *J.B. Andreoli: Stucco decoration. The vault in the Royal Chapel.*

ide of the latter are works by Isidro Arredondo, and depict the two Miracles of San Eloy. These paintings originally came from the Church of the Silversmiths in the no longer existing Madrid parish of San Salvador, from whence they came to form part of the collection of the Marquis of Salamanca, purchased by Isabel II.

Alfonso XII's Billiard Room

We return to the main Gallery and from there enter the first of this suite of María Luisa of Parma's "back-rooms", the name given in the Palace to those rooms in the royal quarters that did not look towards the façades but were interior or received light from the main Courtyard through the Gallery; they were kept for relaxation and private moments aside from the routine of Court life. The ceiling of this room has a fresco painting by Mariano Salvador Maella (1769), with a mythological scene, Juno ordering Aeolus to unleash the Winds against Aeneas. It is undoubtedly the best work in this genre done by this artist, who was still young at the time and who later was perhaps over-prolific, but it is hidden by the wooden coffered ceiling designed by J.S. de Lema when in 1879 Alfonso XII had him build a Billiard Room here: following English Victorian examples and the rationalist derivation of Gothic motifs produced by Viollet-le-Duc, Lema worked here in a manner characteristic of his style and of the taste prevailing in those years; it is perfectly coherent and not without charm, being completed in 1881 and restored in 1993. The joinery and carving of

The Billiard Room of Alfonso XII. ▲

the walnut panelling is by Antonio Girón, as are the other furnishings except for the table, which is from Paris.

Smoking Room or Japanese Room of Alfonso XII

Near the Billiard Room the King wished for a Smoking Room decorated in the Japanese exotic oriental style. Lema covered the walls with bamboo mouldings that hold porcelain plaques ordered from the Boulanger Factory, at Choisy-le-Roi (Paris), and with taffeta panels in blue silk embroidered with Chinese motifs, as seen nowadays following the restoration of 1993; the ensemble had been removed after 1939 due to damage from bombardments during the Civil War. However, it was decided not to replace the ceiling, which was decorated in a similar manner, so as to reveal the eighteenth-century stucco-work and the tempera painting by Joaquín Espalter, dating from 1857.

Queen María Luisa's Stucco Room

Despite its small dimensions, this neoclassical private sitting-room is one of the most fascinating rooms in the Palace. It was designed by Francesco Sabatini and the stucco work is by the Brilli brothers, who found inspiration in the archaeological repertoire of Pompeii then in vogue.

Queen María Luisa's Fine-Woods Room

In evident contrast to the previous room, this private study in the Rococo taste and its furniture (a bureau, two chests-of-drawers, an armchair and two seats) were made by Gasparini's team of cabinetmakers and

The Japanese or Smoking Room of Alfonso XII. ▲

bronzesmiths. It seems to have been one of the private rooms of Charles III, which was dismantled and removed from its original place and adapted to this space in the time of Charles IV. Although the style was already very old-fashioned, the sumptuousness of the work was worthy of the Queen; J.B. Ferroni was responsible for the paving consisting of marble marquetry and for the stucco work on the ceiling, decorated with matching embroidered silk panels on the wall.

Other rooms not included in the visit. The Royal Library

The Rooms of Queen María Luisa and Charles IV

THESE BACK rooms formed part of the Queen's Apartments, the front balconies of which overlook the Plaza de Oriente. Beyond them, the rooms of Charles IV also give onto this square and to the Parade Ground. Of all these rooms that are not open to the public, due to the frequent use made of them by His Majesty the King for his military and civil audiences and other official functions, those particularly worthy of mention are: Queen María Cristina's Saleta, with furniture from the time of Charles IV; the Daily Dining Room, with architectural decoration by Sabatini; Queen María Luisa's Boudoir, also known as the Hall of Mirrors, an exquisite piece of work by the same architect and the same stucco plasterers as the little Plasterwork Room; the Tapestry Room, which takes its name from the tapestries on the History of Joseph, David and Solomon that decorate it; the Weapons Room, with 16th century tapestries; and the Chamber, with large console tables from the reign of Charles III. The ceilings of all these rooms have fresco paintings by F. Bayeu and M. S. Maella, that of the

▲ *Top. The Fine-Woods Room of Queen María Luisa. Below. F. Sabatini: decorative stuccoes, made by the Brilli brothers. A detail from the Hall of Mirrors, the former Boudoir of Maria Luisa of Parma.*

The Stucco Room of Queen Maria Luisa. ▌

Antechamber by Gian Domenico Tiepolo, and that of the Saleta by Gian Battista Tiepolo.

Former Library of Charles IV, subsequently private rooms of the Monarchs in the 19th and 20th centuries.

For the same reasons, there are also no visits to the rooms housed in the St.Giles Wing (between the Parade Ground and Calle Bailén) entered from the Chamber of Charles IV, where this King had his Library, and Isabel II and her successors had their private rooms. The ceilings make up a unitary group of stuccoes and paintings executed between 1784 and 1787, the stuccoes according to Sabatini's designs and the fresco paintings by Bayeu and Maella. The decoration and the furniture correspond to the last period when these rooms were inhabited, during the reign of Alfonso XIII, but include some pieces of great interest from earlier times. There are some remarkable items of 18th-century French and Spanish furniture, a cabinet made of woods from the Indies by Gasparini and chandeliers from the period of Ferdinand VII. It is worthwhile observing, with respect to these rooms, the evolution experienced by the daily life of the Royal Family and royal representation from the Ancien Régime up to the Parliamentary Monarchy: with the changes in customs, and consequently the use of the rooms, the Palace, without growing, began to seem all too big. This change is best illustrated by a rather amusing anecdote told by Edmondo d'Amicis: "When the Bourbons were reigning the entire Palace was occupied: the King lived in the part on the left, towards the Plaza de Oriente; Queen Isabel II in the part facing the Plaza de Oriente on one side and the Plaza de la Armería on the other; Montpensier in the part opposite that of the Queen; each of the Princes had a room facing the Gardens of the Campo del Moro. [It was the

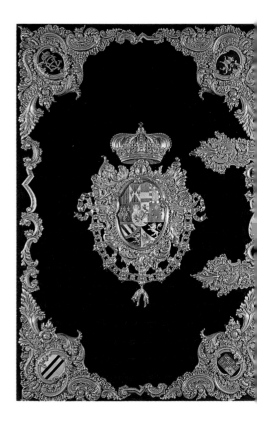

opposite: the King Consort in the rooms of Charles III and in those of the western façade, where the Gala Dining Room is now situated; and the Infantas in the rooms on the east. The wing with the private rooms of Isabel II was the one also occupied later by Alfonso XIII].

During the time that King Amadeus was there, a large part of the building remained empty. He had only three small rooms: one little study, a bedroom and a dressing room. The bedroom gave onto a long passage leading to the rooms of the Princes, beside which were the quarters of the Queen, who never wanted to be separated from her children. There was also a room used for receptions. All this part which served for the entire Royal Family had previously been occupied by Queen Isabel alone. When she heard that King Amadeus and Queen Victoria had satisfied themselves with such a small space

The Binding of the Album presented by La Real Maestranza de Caballería de Sevilla (The Royal Equestrian Order of Seville) to Her Majesty the Queen. 1908. *Velvet, embossed silver and enamels. The Royal Library.*

e is said to have exclaimed in astonishment: "…or young things, they won't be able to move!".

e Royal Library

…e Private Royal Library or His Majesty's …amber Library, as it was called in the 18th …ntury, is not included in the tour. It is located … the lower floor since María Cristina de Borbón …d it moved from the main floor to occupy its …ace with private quarters; its rooms, with …okshelves from the period of Charles III, …bel II and Alfonso XII, have a great deal of …aracter, and the collections of manuscripts and … old printed texts are very important, in …dition to the wealth of illuminated manuscripts …d bindings held there. In the mornings it offers … excellent place for research to be undertaken.

The Lower Floor

FROM THE Main Vestibule, where the gift-shop is located, one goes out to the Small Vestibule of Charles III: the large doorway opposite leads to the suite known since 1924 as the Genoa Rooms. During the Ancien Régime the Ministry of State occupied this area; beyond were the War and Navy Ministries, following the lower gallery around the main Courtyard, at the rear of which was the Ministry of Grace and Justice (where the Library is now situated). Then came the Ministry for the Indies, at the end of the far gallery which continues to the small vestibule of the Chamberlain's Office, opposite the main entrance. Finally, access to the Finance Ministry was by the current entrance to the offices of Patrimonio Nacional beside the Parade Ground. Thus, the essential administrative

A detail from the east apsidal wing with the Royal Coat of Arms by L.S. Carmona, sculpted at the workshop of G.D. Olivieri. ▲
The Main Hallway.

The present building, containing a large hall, was designed by the architects J.S. de Lema and E. Repullés, and was inaugurated 1897. The Collection has been open to the public for over four centuries. The existence a specific guide-book to the Arms Collection makes it unnecessary to provide any further information here.

Royal Pharmacy

THE RANGE of buildings on the opposite side the Parade Ground, where we have come in, houses the Royal Pharmacy, which used to supply medicines to the Royal Family and all the employees and staff of the Royal Household. In the entrance and corridor ther are several large 18th-century Talavera-ware jars. In the first room on the right are display sets of pots and shelving from the pharmacy the former General Hospital of Madrid, also going back to the end of the 18th century. At the end of the corridor, in the second room, there are sets of 18th-century jars from the Royal Pharmacy itself. The third room contai a set of 19th-century porcelain jars, and in the fourth room are 19th-century jars of La Granj crystal. In the last room is a reconstruction of an ancient pharmaceutical "office".

activity of the vast Spanish Monarchy at the moment of its maximum territorial extension was housed on this floor of the Palace.

To reach the Royal Armoury, one goes out to the Parade Ground and follows the gallery of arches on the right, passing the doorway of the General Palace Archive (the most important one in Madrid after the National Historic Archive), with a chance to look out over the landscape extending away as far as the Guadarrama Mountains.

The Royal Armoury

THE ROYAL Armoury of Madrid is the most important armoury in Europe together with the Imperial Armoury in Vienna, due both to the quality of its pieces and the history that confers meaning on such a Collection of Arms, basically intended for gala displays. Philip II ordered it to be moved to the Armoury building, opposite the Alcazar, which stood where the grand railings that enclose the square are now situated.

Surroundings of the Palace

The exterior of the Palace. Plaza de Oriente. Sabatini Gardens. the Park Gardens or "Campo del Moro"

THE PLAZA de la Armería, inserted between th grand railings and the new Cathedral, is narrow and therefore does not offer a perspective of the Royal Palace as distant and

▲ *Filippo and Francesco Negroli: a round shield belonging to Charles V. The Gorgon.* Milan, 1541. *Damascene steel inlaid with gold and silver. The Royal Armoury.*

The Royal Pharmacy: the Baroque herbarium and the range of medicine containers from the old General Hospital of Madrid.

impressive as it would have been if it were not for the triumph, under Alfonso XII, of the idea of using this site (intended since the time of Sacchetti to become a Parade Forecourt) to build the Cathedral of La Almudena, which was finally completed in 1992.

Therefore, in order to enjoy the admirable prospect offered by the Palace from a distance, it is necessary to go to the Plaza de Oriente, an open space created under Joseph Bonaparte by demolishing several buildings of the Royal Household. The site was definitively laid out and landscaped under Isabel II, when the monument with the magnificent Equestrian Statue of Philip IV (by the Florentine sculptor Pietro Tacca) was placed in the centre, opposite the Prince's Gate into the Palace. The balcony

above this jutted out somewhat until Sabatini had it reduced in 1791, taking away the sculpture trophies that it had underneath.

From Calle de Bailén, a flight of steps descends to the Gardens of Sabatini, created during the Second Republic on the site of the Royal Stables built by Sabatini on the instructions of Charles III. The northern façade of the Palace displays here the full height of its various storeys and the Royal Chapel dome.

From these gardens, a ramp goes down to the Paseo de San Vicente, and following the wrought-iron railings as far as the Paseo de la Virgen del Puerto, one reaches the entrance to the Palace Park, popularly known as the Campo del Moro (the Moor's Field). The creation of this historic garden was due to Philip II, and it is

▲ *Pietro Tacca:* Equestrian Statue of Philip IV *in Plaza de Oriente, opposite the Prince's Door.*

◀ *The Northern Façade of the Palace, with the dome of the Royal Chapel, viewed from the Sabatini Gardens.*

greeable though what now exists is less interesting than what was never built. This is because in the 18th century several projects were drawn up, amongst which those of Sacchetti and Ventura Rodríguez, and one commissioned in 1747 from Etienne Boutelou (Head Gardener at Aranjuez) and Garnier de l'Isle (the Superintendant of Versailles), are specially noteworthy. None of them was ever executed, nor was one by Sabatini (1767), but instead it was necessary to wait until the reign of Isabel II, when the project of Narciso Pascual y Colomer (1844) was begun; the design of its main rectilinear avenues still survives, as do the two fountains alined on the central axis, the Fountain of the Shells (by Felipe de Castro and Manuel Álvarez, 1775) brought from the Palace of the

Infante Luis at Boadilla del Monte, and that of the Tritons, an Italian work of the 16th century, brought here from the Islet Garden at Aranjuez and situated in front of the Great Grotto or hothouse. Finally, during the Regency of María Cristina of Habsburg, the park was totally reformed according to a pseudo-landscape design by Ramón Oliva (1890).

The splendid view of Sacchetti's building from the central avenue of the Garden invites us to seek its most spectacular aspect from a more distant point, on the ancient royal property of the Casa de Campo or from the Montaña del Príncipe Pío. Indeed, it is from this perspective, offered by the Royal Seats, that one comes to understand this Royal Palace.

The Western Façade of the Royal Palace of Madrid illuminated at night and seen from the Fountain of Shells ▲ in the Campo del Moro Park.

Bibliography

Alcázar of Madrid

ORSO, Steven N.: *In the presence of the Planet King: Philip IV and the decoration of the Alcázar of Madrid*. Princeton University Press 1986 (revision of doctoral thesis, 1978).

GERARD, Véronique: *De castillo a Palacio. El Alcázar de Madrid en el siglo XVI*. Madrid, Xarait, 1984 (contains the earlier bibliography).

BARBEITO, José: *El Alcázar de Madrid*. Doctoral thesis defended in the Architecture School, Universidad Politécnica de Madrid, 1988. Published by COAM, Madrid 1992.

VARIOUS AUTHORS: *El Real Alcázar de Madrid*. Exhibition Catalogue, by Fernando Checa Cremades. Comunidad de Madrid, 1994.

Guide-Book

NIÑO MAS, Felipe, and JUNQUERA DE VEGA, Paulina: *Guía ilustrada del Palacio Real de Madrid*, Patrimonio Nacional. Madrid, 1956, 3rd ed. This Guide is available in corrected and expanded editions of 1966, by M. López Serrano, and 1985, by F. Fernández-Miranda y Lozana.

General

AGUEDA VILLAR, Mercedes: *Antonio Rafael Mengs 1728-1799*. Exhibition Catalogue, Museo del Prado, Madrid, 1980.

ANDRADA, Ramón: "Las estatuas del Palacio de Oriente vuelven a su sitio", *R.S.*, 1972, 9, Nº 31, pp. 49-56.

ANDRADA, Ramón: "Obras de reconstrucción en el Palacio de Oriente", *R.S.*, 1965, 2, Nº 3, pp. 70-75.

Apollo, LXXXVI, Nº 75, London, May 1968: Special Number on the Royal Palace of Madrid

BARRENO SEVILLANO, Mª Luisa: "Pontifical bordado. Capilla del Palacio Real de Madrid", *R.S.*, 1978, 15, Nº 56, pp. 17-28.

BARRENO SEVILLANO, Mª Luisa: "Salón de Gasparini o pieza de la parada", *R.S.*, 1975, 12, Nº 43, pp. 61-72.

BENITO GARCIA, Pilar: "Los textiles y el mobiliario del Palacio Real de Madrid", *R.S.*, 1991, 28, Nº 109, pp. 45-60.

BOTTINEAU, Yves: *L'Art de Cour dans l'Espagne de Philippe V*, Bordeaux 1962. Spanish ed., *El arte cortesano en la España de Felipe V (1700-1746)*, Madrid, FUE, 1986. New French edition, corrected and expanded, Société des amis du Musée de Sceaux, Paris 1992.

BOTTINEAU, Yves: *L'Art de Cour dans l'Espagne des Lumières*, Paris, De Boccard, 1986.

CABEZA GIL-CASARES, Carmen: "Bordados del salón de Gasparini", *R.S.*, 1992, 29, Nº 114, pp. 12-28.

CABEZA GIL-CASARES, Carmen, and Sancho, José Luis: "La restauración de las salas de billar y de fumar en el Palacio Real de Madrid, la recuperación de un conjunto alfonsino", in *R.S.* Nº 118 (1993).

CHECA CREMADES, Fernando: "Los frescos del Palacio Real Nuevo de Madrid y el fin del lenguaje alegórico", *Archivo Español de Arte*,

XV, 258 (1992), pp.157-178, with complete up-dated bibliography.

COLÓN DE CARVAJAL, José Ramón: *Catálogo de relojes del Patrimonio Nacional*. P.N., Madrid, 1987.

CUMBERLAND, R., *An accurate and descriptive catalogue of the several paintings in the King of Spain's Palace at Madrid*, London, 1787.

DURÁN SALGADO, Miguel: *Exposición de proyectos no realizados relativos al Palacio de Oriente y sus jardines*. Madrid, 1935.

CHALECU, J. Mª, "Los talleres reales de ebanistería, bronces y bordados", *Archivo español de Arte*. 1955, Vol. XXVIII, pp. 237-259.

ESPOZ Y MINA, Condesa de (Juana Vega de Mina): *Apuntes para la historia del tiempo en que ocupó los destinos de aya de S.M. y A. y camarera mayor de Palacio su autora*. Madrid, 1910.

FABRE, Francisco José: *Descripción de las Alegorías pintadas en las bóvedas del Real Palacio de Madrid, hecha de orden de S.M. por ...*, Madrid, Aguado, 1829.

FEDUCHI, Luis M: *Colecciones reales de España: el mueble*. Patrimonio Nacional, Madrid, 1965.

FEDUCHI, Luis M.: *El mueble en España. Volúmenes I y II: El Palacio Nacional*. Madrid, Afrodisio Aguado, 1949.

GARCÍA MERCADAL, J., *Viajes de extranjeros por España y Portugal*. Recopilación, traducción, prólogo y notas por -. Aguilar, Madrid, 1962.

GÓMEZ DE LAS HERAS, *El Palacio Real de Madrid*, Madrid, 1935.

GOMEZ MOLINERO, Encarnación, and SANCHEZ HERNANDEZ, Leticia: "El botamen de cristal de la Real Farmacia. Nuevos datos para su estudio", *R.S.*, 1987, 24, Nº 93, pp. 33-36.

GRITELLA, Gianfranco: *Juvarra. L'Architettura*. Modena, 1992, Vol. II, ficha 124.

IGLESIAS, Helena (dir.): *El Palacio Real de Madrid: un recorrido a través de su arquitectura*. Dibujos de los alumnos de la II Cátedra de Análisis de Formas Arquitectónicas de la ETSAM. Patrimonio Nacional, 1990.

JUNQUERA, Juan José: *La decoración y el mobiliario en los palacios de Carlos IV*. Madrid, 1979.

JUNQUERA, Paulina: "Los libros de coro de la Real Capilla", *R.S.*, 1965, 2, Nº 6, pp. 12-27.

JUNQUERA, Paulina: "Muebles franceses con porcelanas en el Palacio de Oriente", *R.S.*, 1966, 3, Nº 8, pp. 28-37.

JUNQUERA DE VEGA, Paulina, and HERRERO CARRETERO, Concha: *Catálogo de Tapices del Patrimonio Nacional*. Vol. I: siglo XVI. P.N., Madrid, 1986.

JUNQUERA DE VEGA, Paulina, and DÍAZ GALLEGOS, Carmen: *Catálogo de tapices del Patrimonio Nacional*. Vol. II: siglo XVII. P.N., Madrid, 1986.

LÓPEZ SERRANO, Matilde (ed.): *El Palacio Real de Madrid*, Patrimonio Nacional, Madrid, 1975.

MARTÍN, Fernando A.: *Catálogo de la plata del Patrimonio Nacional*. P.N., Madrid 1987.

MORALES Y MARÍN, José Luis: *Mariano Salvador Maella*, Madrid, 1992.

MORALES Y MARÍN, José Luis: *Vicente López (1772-1850)*, Exhibition Catalogue. Madrid, 1990.

MORALES Y MARÍN, José Luis: *Los Bayeu*, Zaragoza, 1979.

MORÁN TURINA, Juan Miguel: *La imagen del Rey. Felipe V y el arte*, Madrid, 1990.

PÉREZ VILLAAMIL, M., *Artes e industrias del Buen Retiro*. Madrid, 1904.

PÉREZ GALDOS, Benito: *La de Bringas*. Madrid, 1884. Ed. Hernando, Madrid.

PLAZA SANTIAGO, Francisco Javier de la: *Investigaciones sobre el Palacio Real Nuevo de Madrid*, Valladolid, 1975. For now this is the fundamental study. It includes all the earlier bibliography.

PONZ, Antonio: *Viaje de España*, XVIII volumenes, Madrid, 1769-1793. Vol.6. 3rd printing, Madrid, Ibarra, 1793.

REYERO, Carlos: "Isabel II y la pintura de historia", *R.S.*, 1991, 28, Nº 107, pp. 28-36.

RUIZ ALCÓN, Mª Teresa: "Habitaciones y objetos personales del rey don Alfonso XIII en el museo del Palacio Real de Madrid", *R.S.*, 1980, 17, Nº 63, pp. 17-28.

SÁNCHEZ HERNÁNDEZ, Leticia: "La vajilla de paisajes del Patrimonio Nacional conservada en el Palacio Real de Madrid", *R.S.*, 1985, 22, Nº 83, pp. 37-52.

SÁNCHEZ HERNÁNDEZ, Mª Leticia: *Catálogo de porcelana y cerámica española del Patrimonio Nacional en los Palacios Reales*. P.N., Madrid, 1989.

SANCHO, José Luis: "Sacchetti y los salones del Palacio Real de Madrid", *R.S.*, 1988, 25, Nº 96, pp. 37-44.

SANCHO, José Luis: "Proyectos del siglo XVIII para los jardines del Palacio de Madrid: Esteban Boutelou y Garnier de *l'Isle*", *Anales del Instituto de Estudios Madrileños*, Vol. XXV (1988) pp. 403-433.

SANCHO, José Luis: "El Palacio Real de Madrid. Alternativas y críticas a un proyecto". Reales Sitios, Special Number (1989), pp. 167-180.

Sancho, José Luis: "El piso principal del Palacio Real", Reales Sitios, Nº 109 (1991).

SANCHO, José Luis: "Fernando Fuga, Nicola Salvi y Luigi Vanvitelli; el Palacio Real de Madrid y sus escaleras principales", in *Storia dell'Arte*, Roma, Nº 72 (1991), pp. 199-252.

SANCHO, José Luis: "Las críticas en España y desde Italia al Palacio Real de Madrid", *Archivo Español del Arte*, Nº 254 (1991), pp. 201-254.

SANCHO, José Luis: "Espacios para la Majestad en el siglo XVIII: la distribución de las habitaciones reales en el Palacio Nuevo de Madrid". *Anales del Instituto de Estudios Madrileños*, Vol. XXXI, Madrid, 1992, pp. 19-40.

SANCHO, José Luis: "Francisco Sabatini, primer arquitecto, director de la decoración interior de los palacios reales", article on pp. 143-166; and notes on interior decoration pp. 227-236, pp. 236-240, pp. 241-244; all in Var.Auth.: *Francisco Sabatini, la arquitectura como metáfora del poder*, Exhibition Catalogue, Madrid, 1993.

SANCHO, José Luis: La arquitectura de los Sitios Reales. *Catálogo histórico de los Palacios, jardines*

Patronatos Reales del Patrimonio Nacional.
Patrimonio Nacional-Fundación Tabacalera,
Madrid, 1995. With complete bibliography and
plans.

TARRAGA BALDO, Mª Luisa: *G.D.Olivieri y el
taller de escultura del Palacio Real.* Patrimonio
Nacional, CSIC and Istituto Italiano de Cultura,
Madrid, 1992.

TORMO 1927: Tormo, Elías: *Las iglesias del
antiguo Madrid.* Madrid,1927. Republished by
Instituto de España. Madrid, 1972.

TURMO, Isabel: *Museo de carruajes.* Patrimonio
Nacional, 1969.

R.S.: *Reales Sitios,* magazine of Patrimonio
Nacional.

THIS BOOK WAS PUBLISHED BY THE NATIONAL
HERITAGE, PRINTED ON 15 TH MARCH 2004,
IN MADRID, AT ESTUDIOS GRÁFICOS EUROPEOS

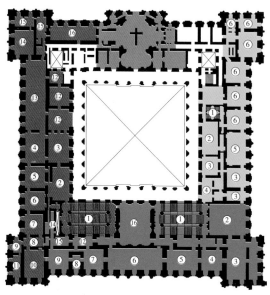

The King's Apartments
1. Staircase
2. Guard Room
3. First Antechamber
4. Second Antechamber
5. Third Antechamber
6. Audience Room
7. The King's Family Room
8. Study
9. The King's Bedroom
12. Back-room
14. Zaguanete Staircase
15. Back Room
16. Ballroom

The Queen's Apartments
1. Staircase
2. Guard Room
3. First Antechamber
4. Second Antechamber
5. Audience Room
6. Family Room
7. Bedroom
8. Passageway to the King's Bedroom

9. The Monarchs' Private Staircase
10. The Queen's Boudoir
11. Private Sitting Room
12. Rooms for Ladies and Servants
13. The Queen's Gallery
14. The Queen's Official Bedroom
15. Private Sitting Rooms
16. Area leading to Royal Gallery in Chapel

Apartments of the Prince and Princess
1. The Prince's Staircase
2. Guard Room
3. Antechambers
4. Servants' Staircase and Rooms
5. Audience Room
6. Private Rooms

Distribution of the Main Floor of the Palace under Charles III, (1759-1788), after the modifications introduced by Sacchetti in 1760

The King's Apartments
1. Main Staircase
2. Guard Room
3. Ballroom
4. Anteroom
5. Audience Room
6. Saleta or the King's Luncheon Room
7. Antechamber, or the King's Dining Room
8. Chamber or Dressing Room
9. Study or Woods-of-the-Indies Room
10. Oratory
11. Bedroom
12. Small room

The Queen's Apartments
(occupied by the Infanta María Josefa from 1766)
1. First Antechamber
2. Second Antechamber
3. Dining and Audience Room
4. Chamber
5. Bedroom
6. Small room

The Prince's Apartments
1. Tricks or Billiard Room, or Saleta

2. The Prince's Dining Room
3. Small rooms
4. Dressing Room
5. Bedroom of the Prince and Princess

The Princess's Apartments
6. First Antechamber
7. Second Antechamber
8. Third Antechamber
9. Audience Room of the Prince and Princess
10. The Princess's Conversation Room and Boudoir
11. Small rooms of the Princess
12. The Prince's Staircase

The Infantes' Quarters
Apartments of the Infante Gabriel (formerly of Infante Luis) and of Infanta María Ana Victoria
1. First Antechamber
2. Second Antechamber, the Infante's Dining Room
3. Sala
4. Dressing Room
5. Bedroom
6. (Chinese) Boudoir
7. Small room

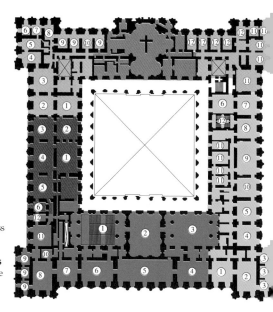

8. Room of the Birds
9. Rooms of the Infanta María Ana Victoria
10. Ladies' Room
11. Apartments of the Infanta María Josefa until 1776, then of the sons of Charles IV

12. Apartments of the Infante Antonio, then of the sons of Charles IV. The Infante Pedro and Francisco Javier had their quarters on the second floor